*In humble dedication to those brave me*
*of the Bristol Channel who, with their stout*
*boats, went seeking 'Downalong'*

The ex-Newport yawl *Mascotte*, built by Cox in 1904 and now fully restored. [courtesy Tony Winter]

# THE SAILING PILOTS
# OF THE BRISTOL CHANNEL

PETER J. STUCKEY

redcliffe

First published in 1977 by David & Charles

This revised and enlarged edition first published in 1999 by
Redcliffe Press Ltd, 81g Pembroke Road, Bristol BS8 3EA

Reprinted 2010


www.redcliffepress.co.uk
info@redcliffepress.co.uk

© Peter J Stuckey

ISBN 978-1-906593-64-3

British Library Cataloguing-in-Publication Data
A catalogue record for this book is available from the British Library

Cover design by Mark Cavanagh
Printed by MPG Books Ltd, Bodmin, Cornwall

# CONTENTS

# Foreword

This is the first book ever written about the Bristol Channel pilot cutters and the men who worked them. It contains not only exact details of construction and design but beautiful stories of an era only just within living memory of a few. 'There's nothing so certain in pilotage, my son, as the uncertainty of it.' This was said to me by a senior member of my piloting family when I was a very new apprentice at the age of 15; and of course it meant little to me then.

I have no doubt that my elder was really referring to the days related in this book, yet the saying holds good today for many pilots in these ever changing times.

While it may not be any good living in the past, it is often very pleasant to contemplate; and within these covers Peter Stuckey takes a hard factual look at the circumstances and the times of the men and boats of the Bristol Channel pilotage services in the days when they literally had to 'out punt' to earn their living.

**John Rich, Bristol Channel pilot**

# Introduction to the second edition
## 1999

Since the publication of the first edition much new material has come to light, with older readers having had their memories stimulated to recall personal connections with the pilotage services, either first-hand or through family traditions. In fact, over twenty years, interest in the subject has expanded dramatically, from one of mild enthusiasm by 'traditional' sailing types and appreciation among other sea-goers, to an explosion of fascination over a much wider field. In the United Kingdom, the U.S.A. and Canada original pilot cutters, thought to be ending their days as house-boats or hulks, are in the process of being restored to full sailing commission – most of them even sporting their original working numbers and sail markings! Such is the concern for accuracy.

Full scale copies are being built to original line drawings and new craft being built on Bristol Channel Pilot cutter lines, such as the 'Westernman' being produced in numbers by Covey Island Boatworks in Nova Scotia and at least one builder in Germany.

They have also caught the imagination of the model builders and many model boating lakes can now boast a veritable fleet – every boat rivalling its neighbour for accuracy of detail!

In view of this I felt that a second edition was called for, firstly because it gave me an opportunity to make minor corrections to the text as a result of the influx of new material, secondly to add to the existing personal anecdotes and thirdly to include a short chapter on modern restoration on original craft, with another on the serious modelling of these magnificent vessels. For the latter I am grateful to the shipwrights and eminent model-makers for their unstinting co-operation in putting these chapters together.

Likewise I am greatly indebted to all who have given so freely of their knowledge and their permission to use treasured documents and photographs. I trust that they will consider their generosity adequately rewarded.

P.J.S. 1999

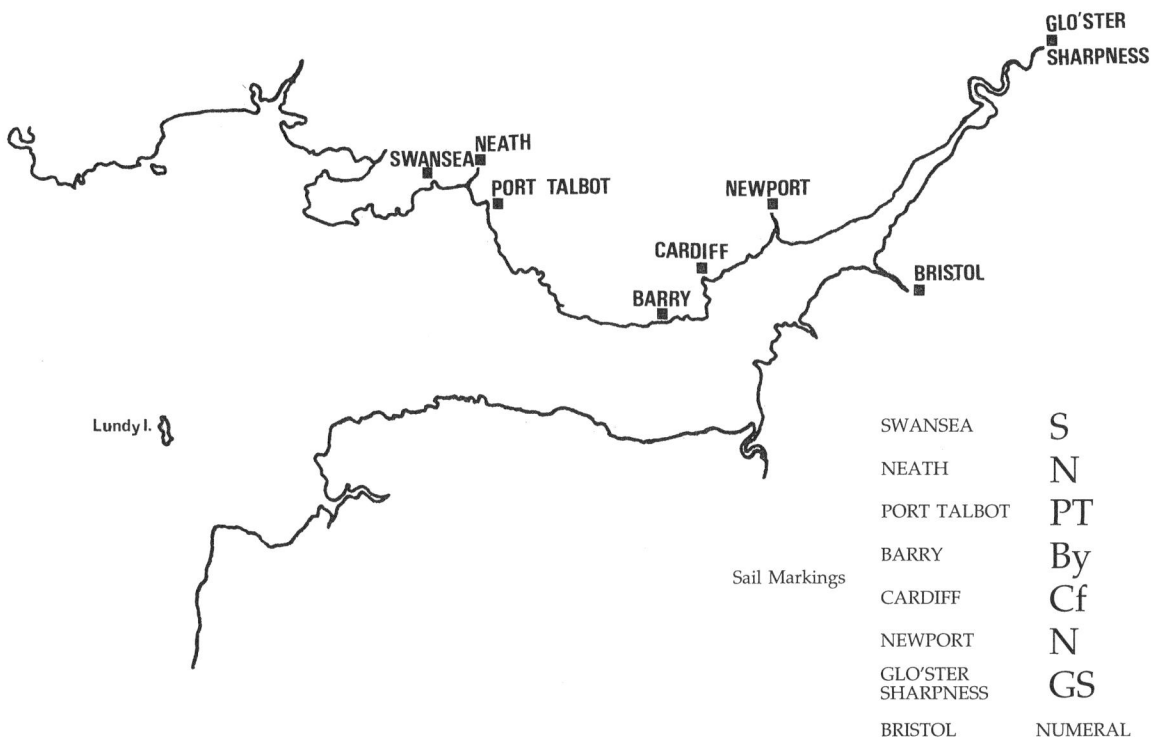

| | |
|---|---|
| SWANSEA | S |
| NEATH | N |
| PORT TALBOT | PT |
| BARRY | By |
| CARDIFF | Cf |
| NEWPORT | N |
| GLO'STER SHARPNESS | GS |
| BRISTOL | NUMERAL |

Sail Markings

*Fig 1*  The Pilot Ports of the Bristol Channel

# CHAPTER ONE

# The Origin of the Pilot Service

According to a tradition among Bristol pilots as yet unsupported by documentary evidence, James George Ray – master of a barge employed in victualling the forts at the mouth of the Avon – was the 'official' Bristol Channel pilot, having been appointed in May 1497 by the Mayor and Corporation for the express purpose of piloting John Cabot's *Matthew*. He was joined in that office by James Shepherd, another barge-master, later in the same year.

This particular tradition may be unsubstantiated but there is no doubt that the Rays have figured in more than one of the great moments in Bristol's maritime history. In 1837, for instance, it was Pilot George Ray (*Waterwitch*, No 24) who guided the pioneer Atlantic steamship *Great Western* safely out into open water, while William Ray (*Triumph*, No 14) piloted the larger *Great Britain* in 1844.

There is also conclusive evidence to show that in the year 1611 control of the pilotage was delegated by Bristol Corporation to the Society of Merchant Venturers of Bristol, who were to retain control of it for two and a half centuries. The precise area over which the Bristol Corporation claimed the right to appoint pilots is not clearly defined but the inference is that they assumed responsibility for the greater part of the Bristol Channel. To quote from Grahame Farr's historical notes on Bristol Channel Pilotage:

> At first, no doubt, the matter was not questioned owing to the obvious ascendancy of the port, but in the course of time the Channel was divided by authority of Exchequer Warrants under various 'Head Ports' for fiscal purposes, and it seems that towards the end of the eighteenth century their growing pains caused agitation for some statement of policy on pilotage. Two of the more important Bristol Harbour Acts, 11 and 12 William III c.23, (1756), and 43 George III c.140 (1803), defined the pilotage area by stating simply that the Mayor, Aldermen and Common Council were to 'appoint any Person or Persons duly qualified for that Purpose to be and officiate as Pilot or Pilots within the Port of Bristol.'

This was decidedly misleading, for the outer limits of the Customs Port were then the shoreline from King Road to Uphill, thereafter following imaginary straight lines drawn to Steep Holm, Flat Holm, Aust and then back along the shore of the Severn to King Road. This, of course, did not cover any of the South Wales ports nor any other important landing place in the Bristol Channel.

According to one historian, Swansea pilotage became independent by virtue of the Swansea Harbour Act of 1791 (31 George III c.83), which contained provisions for the newly elected trustees to appoint pilots for their own bay and port, but they may ultimately have been subject to Bristol, as will be seen later.[1] For other places the position was not so clearly defined and Chappell, writing of Cardiff, states:

> Up to the end of the 18th Century there was no local pilotage and no standard of skill or efficiency was enforced on persons engaged in the responsible task of guiding vessels in and out of the harbours of the Bristol Channel. In 1798 steps were taken to institute a system of control and the Bristol Corporation was constituted the Pilotage Authority, not only for the Severn ports but also for ports farther west, including Cardiff. The powers do not appear to have been fully applied locally and the five pilots who served Cardiff in 1806 were apparently subject to no special authority. A minute of the Cardiff Town Council of 23 June of that year records a report of the Town Clerk that pilotage control was vested in the Corporation but was not exercised. Four months later, however, it was reported that a search of the Town Charters had been made and that these gave the Corporation no control over pilots.[2]

I have found no trace of the regulation of 1798 but the position was clarified by the Bristol Channel Pilotage Act (47 George III c.33) which received Royal assent on 1 August 1807. The preamble to this Act stated:

> Whereas the Mayor, Burgesses and Commonalty of the City of Bristol by ancient Charters and Grants from the Crown, have been for several hundred Years past Owners of the Port of Bristol, with several Creeks and Harbours in the Bristol Channel as Members thereof: and the said Corporation are Conservators of the Rivers within the said Port from a certain Place about Four Miles Eastward of King Road and so down the River Severn and Bristol Channel to the two small islands called the Stipe Holmes and the Flat Holmes . . . (and) have from Time to Time appointed Persons to be and officiate as Pilots within the Port of Bristol, and Jurisdiction aforesaid . . . (their authority shall) be extended to the Appointment of Pilots for the conducting of Ships and Vessels into and out of and upon the whole of the Bristol Channel, and the several Ports, Harbours and Creeks belonging to and issuing from the same . . . (that

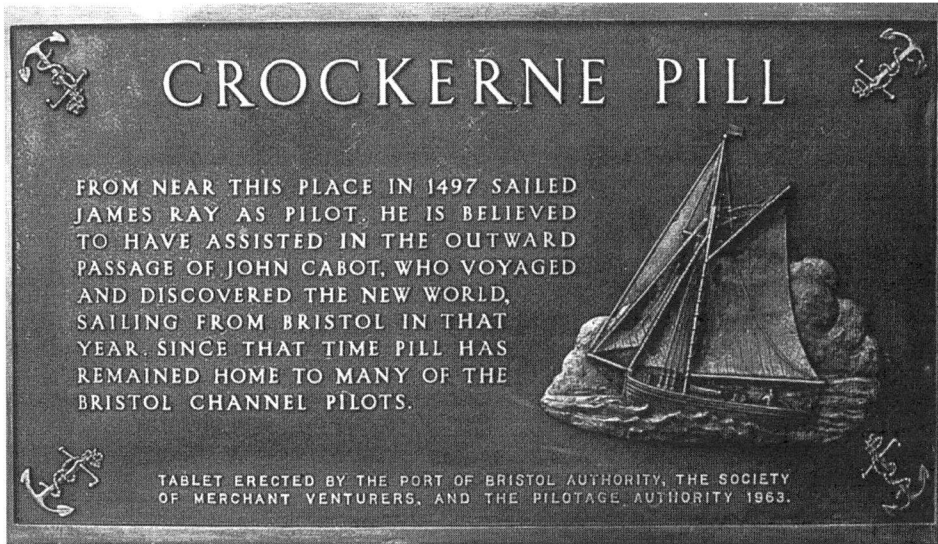

CROCKERNE PILL

FROM NEAR THIS PLACE IN 1497 SAILED
JAMES RAY AS PILOT. HE IS BELIEVED
TO HAVE ASSISTED IN THE OUTWARD
PASSAGE OF JOHN CABOT, WHO VOYAGED
AND DISCOVERED THE NEW WORLD,
SAILING FROM BRISTOL IN THAT
YEAR. SINCE THAT TIME PILL HAS
REMAINED HOME TO MANY OF THE
BRISTOL CHANNEL PILOTS.

TABLET ERECTED BY THE PORT OF BRISTOL AUTHORITY, THE SOCIETY
OF MERCHANT VENTURERS, AND THE PILOTAGE AUTHORITY 1963.

Bronze tablet, designed by the author, marking the role played by Pill in the
pilotage story.

Pill creek and Rowles' yard. The steam tug passing the entrance might
be the *Fury*. Artist unknown, but painting probably c.1850.

A group of pilots and westernmen at Pill about 1880. [courtesy Port of Bristol Authority]

is) all Vessels passing up and down and upon the Bristol Channel to and from the Eastward of Lundy Island, and in or upon the several creeks of the said Channels.

This Act came into force on 1 October 1807 and byelaws for the conduct of pilots were drawn up and published in 1809, further regulations being issued from time to time, notably in 1840 and 1853.[3]

Although doubt of authority no longer existed, the position of the smaller but growing Bristol Channel Ports was still obviously unsatisfactory. In October 1836 Cardiff town council asked Bristol to allow them to appoint their own pilots but were rebuffed.[4] In March 1840 they sought Parliamentary powers, but failed, yet by October 1860 the number of Cardiff pilots had increased to forty, which was but few less than those of Bristol. In the following year Cardiff, Newport and Gloucester took concerted action and succeeded in getting Parliament to pass a new Bristol Channel Pilotage Act which gave them the independence they sought. In the reorganisation that followed this measure the Society of Merchant Venturers relinquished its interest and Bristol pilots were thereafter appointed directly by the Bristol Corporation.

Of the other ports in the Bristol Channel, Bridgwater had apparently been made an independent pilotage authority some time before 1861. Bideford and Barnstaple, although east of Lundy, appear never to have come under the control of Bristol, which is not altogether surprising since, fiscally, they had been connected with the port of Exeter for several centuries, even when Bristol was the head port for the rest of the Channel. As regards Swansea, also east of Lundy, one concludes that the Act of 1791 was altered in respect of pilots by the uncompromising wording of the 1807 Act. Certainly the *Shipping Gazette* of a date early in 1854 stated: 'The Bristol Town Council are naturally anxious to maintain the monopoly which they now enjoy of appointing pilots for the whole Channel, but we think Swansea in particular, is a port of sufficient importance to have a voice in the matter. Barry was given its own pilotage authority by its Dock Act of 1885, and a Port Talbot authority was later created.'[5]

So much for the origins and structure of the pilot service in the days of sail, but what of the men of those early years who prized so highly their title of 'pilot', and of the sturdy craft in which they went seeking 'Downalong'?

Unquestionably, the vast majority of these pilots belonged to the ancient village of Crockerne, or Crewkerne Pill, and they held the City of Bristol in no very high regard, even though they were administered by the Society of Merchant Venturers. Grievances – imaginary or otherwise – gave rise to a tradition of hostility which can be detected even today, their intense pride of community not having been in the least diminished.

One old pilot writing of his beloved Crewkerne Pill goes so far as to accuse the city of suppressing the history of Pill out of sheer malice, whilst that of the surrounding districts is given full coverage in all the guide-books. He attributes this to an age-old jealousy 'between the city and the village which has always supplied the city with its pilots but which Bristol has never been able to bring beneath its authority'.

The men of Bristol traditionally regarded the pilots and seamen of Pill as 'sharks', and certainly they were no more saintly than the city merchants who traded in 'black ivory', or sent leaky ships to sea with crews on starvation rations. There is also evidence that, in Lancastrian days, the men of Pill went 'a-pirating' with the rest. Our old pilot writes of '. . . certain men of Pill who stole a barque and went a-pirating. Some time later they were foolish enough to return to Pill, where they were arrested and hanged by their feet from the bridge opposite Prince Street at low tide. Thus if they did not first die of apoplexy, they were doomed to watch their death approach inch by inch. The barbarity of the punishment shows perhaps the feeling that existed between Bristol and Pill men at a time when piracy was not a particularly heinous crime . . .'

Smuggling was also a profitable sideline to piloting and 'The revenue officer was kept busy in the old days when nearly every man in Pill used to go "Westerning". Silks, spirits and tobacco used to find their way in without paying a ha'porth of duty . . .' And this at a time when a customs and revenue smack had its station within sight of Pill, in King Road!

Until its development in recent years, Pill was a village of narrow alleyways which must have witnessed many a contraband cargo being smuggled into the deep cellars under the old houses. It is even said that a man might go into one house by the front door and, after a few twists and turns, find himself coming out of a neighbour's back door! A quaint legend as to the origin of Pill has it that back in the distant past an Irish cobbler of neighbouring Easton-in-Gordano ordered a cargo of shoes or, in the Gaelic, 'brogues', instead of which a shipload of 'rogues' was landed and became the founders of Pill.

Of its later and more turbulent days Grahame Farr comments: 'In the old days discipline seems to have been good on the whole, although the Press sometimes records cases of suspension.' For instance, in the *Bristol Mirror* of 1 September 1810, it was stated:

> John Brown, the pilot who ran the Rosetti on shore, which ship was totally lost, was broke last week by the Company of Merchants and thereby rendered incapable of serving again in that capacity for neglect of duty, carelessness, obstinacy and ignorance. It is hoped that this will make the pilots in general more attentive and less insolent.

Despite this scathing report, John Brown's suspension could only have been of a temporary nature for he is shown in the list of pilots for each year from 1809 to 1837.

A similar case occured in 1851 when John Percival was suspended for six months for stranding the recently completed steamship *Demerara* in the Avon, though contemporary press reports of the incident lead one to suspect that the pilot had to take the blame for bad judgement on the part of the tug-master.

If the men of Pill earned themselves a reputation, so did their boats as the heavily built, apple-cheeked craft of the seventeenth to early nineteenth centuries gradually evolved into the splendid cutters of the early twentieth century, admired the world over by professional and amateur sailors alike. A Bristol pilot cutter was always referred to as a 'skiff', whilst the Welsh boats were known as 'yawls', even though they were cutter-rigged and often built in Bristol or at Pill. In his book *Boats and Boatmen*, T.C. Lethbridge suggests that the term 'skiff' or 'skarf' is derived from the Roman 'scafa' (a small boat), and it is certainly true that the term 'skiff' is used to describe a variety of small craft from the south of England to western Scotland. But whatever the origin, a Bristol pilot's boat has been known as a 'skiff' as long as records have been kept and for the purpose of this book I am content to leave it at that.

Up to the eighteenth century we are sadly lacking any detailed description of the craft used by the pilots but the following extract from Grahame Farr's notes on Bristol Channel pilotage is helpful, as are his footnotes.

> Diligent search has failed to produce pictorial evidence of the type of craft employed by the Bristol pilots in the eighteenth century and earlier. It may be suggested that before the 1807 Act regularised the profession and increased the number of pilots, thereby increasing the competition, they were small open boats.
>
> However, this is shown to be unlikely by evidence contained in a 'Register of Ships' commenced in 1795 by the Corporation of Bristol under authority of the Act 35 George III, c.58.[6] The Act was intended for river craft and the local registry covered 'all Lighters, Barges, Boats, Wherries and other vessels exceeding the burthen of Thirteen Tons. . . . Worked, Rowed or Navigated in or upon the Rivers, Canals and other Inland Waters or Navigations within the City of Bristol and County of the Same City'. It is a little surprising that pilot skiffs are listed, for in their case, under a column headed 'Area of Employment' is a statement of which the following is typical: 'Navigation from Pill in the County of Somerset, up the River Avon to Bristol and from Pill the whole extent of the Bristol Channel and occasionally into the English Channel, St George's Channel and to Ireland, the number of miles uncertain.' The particulars given for the twelve skiffs are here reproduced and it will be seen that some of the present-day pilot families are represented.[7]

Bristol pilot skiff *Trial* (Pilot T Vowles, 1847-78) with hatch cover abaft the mast. She may have doubled as a fishing boat. [courtesy PBA]

| Reg No | Name | Tons | Master's name | No of men employed | Capacities |
|--------|------|------|---------------|--------------------|------------|
| 3 | *Success* | 24 | Peter Seavell, Jr | Samuel Cox | Mariner |
| | | | | Thomas Tippet | Apprentice |
| 6 | *James and Samuel* | 14 | James Craddy, Jr | William Lockyear | Mariner |
| | | | | John Rowland | Mariner |
| 7 | *Harbinger* | 19 | Samuel Spear | Thomas Rumley | Mariner |
| | | | | John Haskins | Apprentice |
| 8 | *Polly* | 18 | John Webber | John Hall | Mariner |
| | | | | John Hyde | Apprentice |
| 9 | *Elizabeth* | 15 | James Scarretts | Charles Mantle | Mariner |
| | | | | Samuel Shepherd | Apprentice |
| | | | | William Harris | Apprentice |
| 10 | *Royal William* | 14 | George Parfitt | Thomas Ray | Mariner |
| | | | | William Owen | Apprentice |
| 13 | *Star* | 18 | Thomas Hammer | Joseph Hazle | Mariner |
| | | | | William Kington | Mariner |
| | | | | Samuel Brooks | Apprentice |
| 14 | *Resolution* | 14 | Samuel Cole | James Rogers | Mariner |
| | | | | James Harris | Boy |
| 15 | *Ann* | 14 | Joseph Cox | John Hall | Mariner |
| 16 | *Endeavour* | 15 | George Thayer | Benjamin Browne | Mariner |
| | | | | Thomas Thayer | Boy |
| 20 | *Betsy* | 19 | James Payne | Samuel Hanmore | Mariner |
| | | | | Samuel Hazard | Apprentice |
| 40 | *Hero* | 23 | John Gilmore | William Gilmore | Mariner |
| | | | | Thomas Jones | Boy |

It is probable that most of the pilot skiffs were also registered with the Customs authorities under the Act 26 George III, c.60 (1786), which was the first Act to make possible the universal registration of British shipping. The Act was intended for 'vessels of Fifteen Tons and Upwards, having a deck . . .' but in practice the privilege of registration was often sought and received by owners of smaller vessels. The earliest surviving registration records for Bristol are the duplicate oaths for the years 1814 to 1820 and 1822, and the original books are intact from 1824. In searching these records I was able to trace five eighteenth-century craft which were in use as pilot skiffs, although it cannot be said with certainty that they were built for the purpose. As their dimensions and main historical data are of interest, they are listed below.[8]

*William and Jane*: Built at Bristol in 1768, rebuilt in 1789, and lengthened in 1831. She was listed as a pilot skiff 1837–45 (James Rowland) and broken up in 1852. In a register of 1825 she was owned by John

Rowland, mariner; tonnage 18, dimensions 36ft × 11ft 2in × 5ft 5in. After 1831 she measured 20 tons, dimensions 36ft 9in × 11ft 6¾in × 5ft 9½in.

*Betsy*: Built at Bristol in 1786. A register of 1814 shows her owned by Thomas Shepherd, mariner (he had been a pilot at least since 1801), and she was listed as a pilot skiff between 1837 and 1840 (James Ray), after which she was sold to Barnstaple. The register shows her tonnage to be 21, and dimensions as 39ft 8in × 11ft 6in × 6ft 6in.

*Bristol Endeavour*: Built at Pill in 1791. A register of 1817 refers to an earlier register in 1805 which was cancelled when the vessel sank in Morgan's Pill, but she had then been raised and repaired. She was owned by James Buck, pilot, but sold in the same year and afterwards sunk in the Channel. Her tonnage was 16, and dimensions 37ft 2in × 10ft 4in × 5ft. Possibly she is identical with the *Endeavour* of the 1795 register.

*Tartar*: Built at Bristol in 1794. In a register of 1816 she was owned by George Thayer, pilot (he was appointed in this) and was apparently broken up soon afterwards. Tonnage 21, and dimensions 36ft 4in × 12ft 2in × 6ft.

*Fancy*: Built at Bristol in 1796 as an open boat; rebuilt and decked in 1801. In 1825 she was owned by James Parfitt, pilot, and was broken up in 1831. Tonnage 13, and dimensions 33ft 9in × 9ft 8in × 5ft 9in.

One other fragment completes our present knowledge of eighteenth-century Bristol pilot craft. This is a report of a loss in 1790 which reads 'Loss of the *Swan* pilot skiff. Saturday, the 26th ult, the *Swan* pilot-boat being on shore of the Holmes-Kidwell, the owner, in endeavouring to get her off at the first of flood, the wind being WNW a great surf dashed her to pieces against a rock, whereby the owner was unfortunately drowned.[9]

For the greater part of the nineteenth century Bristol pilot craft are well documented. The 1807 Act did not lay down rules for the size of skiffs but was content to stipulate the markings to be carried: 'Each pilot's skiff shall be marked with the number appointed for her by the havenmaster, in black paint on the three lower sails, such number to be at least four feet in length; the hull to be painted black, with a white streak under the gunwhale; to be also numbered on the bow and the pilot's name on the stern, and to carry a flag constantly at the mast-head, with blue and white horizontal stripes, of the dimensions four feet by five feet.[10] This flag was eventually superseded by the present one of white over red equally divided horizontally.

Grahame Farr continues:

By a stroke of good fortune there have been preserved the lines of the skiff *Charlotte*, built by the Hilhouses of Bristol in 1808 for John Berry, pilot. The plans, drawn up by George Hilhouse, have been preserved among others by Charles Hill & Sons, ship-builders and successors to the Hilhouses.[11] This skiff was a medium-bodied little craft with a forefoot rather shallower than in later examples. She had a clean run except that it was slightly interrupted by the tuck under her square stern. Her timbers give the impression of great strength. Dimensions given on the plans are: length from the forepart of the stern aloft to the afterpart of the post on the keel, 33ft 2in: length extreme aloft 38ft, breadth extreme 11ft 8in, depth from skin to skin 6ft 4½in, admeasurement 1888/94 tons: mast (including 7ft head) 43ft, boom 32ft 9in, gaff 20ft, bowsprit 34ft.

There is no sail plan of the *Charlotte*, but the spar dimensions are a help in this matter and the following advertisement, dated 1812, gives a clue to the sails and equipment carried by skiffs of the period: 'For Sale, the skiff *James and Samuel*, 14½ tons, at Pill, with furniture, etc. consisting of 2 anchors, 2 cables, 1 mainsail, 2 foresails, 4 jibs, 1 squaresail, 1 gaff-topsail, 1 topmast-steering sail, 1 pont [sic]- James Craddy, sr.'[12]


## AUTHOR'S NOTE

I am greatly indebted to the Bristol marine historian, Grahame Farr, and to Pilot H.B. Watkins for much of the information contained in this chapter.


## NOTES

1. Jones, W.H. *The History of the Port of Swansea* (Carmarthen: Spurell & Son, 1922), p.295.
2. Chappell, E.L., *History of the Port of Cardiff* (Cardiff: Priory Press, 1939), p.117.
3. The 1809 Rules were published as 'bye-laws, rules and orders . . . for . . . pilots, watermen and others . . . within the Port of Bristol and within the Bristol Channel to the eastward of Lundy Island'. The fees for pilotage from Lundy to King Road were at this time: under 100 tons, 3 guineas; 100–200 tons, 4 guineas; 200–300 tons, 5 guineas; 300 tons and upwards, 6 guineas.
4. Chappell, E.L., op cit, p.117.
5. Quoted in *Bristol Mirror*, 14 January 1854.

6.   Bristol Civic Archives (Inv No 05077/1). Unfortunately, the register was not kept up to date and there are only 44 entries; 43 dated 1795 and one dated 1802.

7.   The term 'skiff' rather than 'cutter' was always used in the service in the days of sail. Its origin in this connection merits investigation. Possibly such craft were generally skiffs in the days when cutters, whether naval, revenue or packet, were sizeable craft of advanced rig. Almostly certainly the term is a relic of the days when the class of a craft was determined by her hull form rather than the rig of her masts.

8.   Copies from the Registers by permission of the Commisioners of Customs and Excise.

9.   *Felix Farley's Bristol Journal*, 10 July 1790.

10.   In 1861, when other pilotage authorities were created in the Bristol Channel, the Port of Bristol pilots retained the number in the main-sail while other ports adopted initials such as 'By' 'Cf ', etc. Numbers on present pilot craft are station numbers. For instance, the Bristol craft are number 1 on the Breaksea station; 2, at Portishead; 3, reserve; 4 and 5, tenders to No 2.

11.   Hillhouse Draughts, fo. 41. Also Science Museum (Kensington) negative 5954.

12.   *Bristol Mirror*, 28 November 1812.

# CHAPTER TWO

# The Boats

The dimensions of an average Bristol Channel pilot cutter at the turn of the century was of the order of 40 to 50ft overall, with a beam of 10 to 11ft and a draught of 7 to 10ft at the heel. Specific details of such a vessel, the *Hilda*, have been provided by Capt. H. Watkins, who served his apprenticeship in her from 1908. She was built by Cooper of Pill in 1899 in six months with the assistance of one boy and at a cost of about £350 – inclusive of hull, blocks, spars and ballast.

| | |
|---|---|
| Length overall | 49ft 0in |
| Length on load water line | 43ft 0in |
| Breadth | 13ft 5in |
| Draught at heel | 8ft 0in |
| Freeboard at bow | 5ft 0in |
| Freeboard at stern | 2ft 9in |
| Minimum freeboard | 2ft 3in |
| Depth of bulwark | 1ft 6in |

The ballast consisted of concrete between the floors, plus movable iron pigs, whereas when another cutter, the *Pet*, built by Rowles in 1904, was broken up at the Underfall Yard in Bristol in 1965, an artillery shell was discovered concreted into her ballast and a bomb disposal squad had to be brought in to remove it.

Capt. Watkins also describes the typical construction of a pilot skiff of this period:

The keel was 6in thick, varying in depth to 18in, 40 or more feet long of elm and in one piece. Stem and stern posts were of oak. Grown oak frames were from 4 × 3in to 6 × 3in, double amidships and single at the ends. Planking was of oak, elm and pitch-pine 1¾ in to 2in thick in varying widths, with decks of pine 1¾ to 2 × 3¼in wide. The mast was of pitch-pine or Oregon pine with pine spars.

The widely spaced shrouds – three per side – and all other standing rigging, was of wire. Most craft had their shrouds set up with dead-eyes and lanyards although a few were fitted with rigging screws. All

*Out Punt*, painting by the author. [courtesy Brian Taber]

running gear was of the best manilla and all blocks were fitted with patent sheaves.

Cotton sails were used for summer and flax for winter work. In the case of Bristol boats, the pilot's number was painted on one side of the mainsail and on the opposite side of the foresail, whereas the Welsh and Gloucester-Sharpness craft displayed only the initial letter in capitals, with the final letter of the port's name in lower case, except that the Gloucester-Sharpness boats did not include the small letter but displayed only the 'G-S'. The regulations called for sail markings to be 'not less than three feet in length' and the Bristol vessels were required to show them in 'the three lower sails', although in practice they seemed to be confined to mainsail and foresail only.

It was a common requirement on both sides of the Bristol Channel that the pilot craft be painted black, both topsides and below the waterline, although a coloured boot-topping was permitted. The Gloucester-Sharpness boats, however, were distinctive in having a white bulwark: a distinction carried on to the present day. On the bulwark, just forward of the shrouds, was painted the pilot's number and the boat's name was carried across the stern together with the pilot's name and the name of his port in white on all but G-S boats which, of course, reversed the colours. The G-S craft alone sometimes used Roman numerals, which must have made identification difficult at times.

As from 1 March 1849 all pilot vessels were required to fly at the masthead a flag 'of large dimensions' divided horizontally, the upper half being white and the lower half red. At night, she had to show an all-round white light at the the masthead when working and a kerosene flare every fifteen minutes. Each port had its own flare code – long, two shorts and a long for Bristol, long and short for Cardiff, long and three shorts for Barry etc. The flare can was a metal container tapering from about 10in diameter at the base to about 3 or 4 in diameter at the neck. A wad of cotton waste was attached to a handle with a circular handshield which served also as a lid for the can. The wad, soaked in kerosene, would be lit and held aloft as required, using the mainsail as a reflector (Fig 2). From the year 1858 all sailing craft were obliged to show sidelights when under way at night – in accordance with the Merchant Shipping Act of 1854 – but few, if any, Bristol Channel pilot craft ever complied with this, showing only their all-round white light, whether working or not.

The deck layout was simple and clean, free of raised skylights or other obstructions which might impair the easy handling of the gear or the boarding punt. Daylight was admitted below by flush deadlights in the deck. Ventilation to the living-quarters was not high on the list of priorities, for men whose daily lives were on deck had a surfeit of fresh air.

From forward to aft the main features on deck were first, the bitt-heads – enormous baulks of timber standing high above the bulwarks and passing down through the

Cf.By. No.20 *Annie M* and No.42 (*Amanda*?) off Penarth, 1896. [courtesy National Maritime Museum]

*Fig 2*   Signal flare can, as used by pilots

deck to the keelson. There were usually three bitt-heads, the centre and starboard ones providing a location for the heel of the reefing bowsprit, which passed through a hole in the bulwark to the starboard side of the stem. A heel-rope tackle was secured to these two timbers.

Between the port and centre bitt-heads was the anchor windlass, the anchor itself being stowed on the port side and its cable hawsehole piercing the bulwark to port of the stem post. In fact, the bitts often look out of proportion to the size of the cutter until one remembers that, with the advent of steam, it was not unusual for the pilot craft to be taken in tow by a ship once the pilot was on board so that she would be back on station when the job was completed. Once the cutter was in tow, the ship would proceed at her normal speed so that the strain on the cutter's bitt-heads was tremendous and would have pulled a lesser craft in two. The evidence of this sort of towing can be seen in the grooves cut into the bitt timbers of any of the surviving cutters whose original bitts remain. Pilot Frank Trott's famous *Marguerite* actually had a genuine tug's towing hook fitted to the fore side of the bitts especially for this purpose.

Towing was obviously a great time-saver for the pilot, who would otherwise have had to wait for his cutter to catch him up in port if inward bound, or to arrange a

Cutter *Cymro* towing to Nash Point with Pilot Frank Trott. Note the 'double licence' markings in mainsail. Towing was not popular with crews. [courtesy N Alexander]

The skiff *Petrel* at Pill (Pilot G F Dickens) 1899-1901. The flag hoist
suggests that she had been newly launched. [courtesy PBA]

The cutter *Rhoda* in tow of the Norwegian barque *Asta*. She is unusually displaying the Bristol number 18 in the foresail and the Cardiff CF in the main. This suggests the pilot has a double licence.

Bristol pilot skiffs about 1910, including No.23 *Britton* (W G Ray) in foreground and No.7 *Victoria* (Edwin H A Carey) third from left. Rowles' Pill yard is in the background. [PBA]

rendezvous somewhere 'down-a-long' if outward bound. But it was hated by the crew members who, tough though they were, found it an exhausting job to keep the boat under control at speed, with the foredeck under green water up to the mast for hours at a time. Most of them would much rather have sailed the distance into the teeth of a gale.

Just abaft the bitts and slightly to port was the fore-hatch which gave access to the foc's'le and forepeak; then, a little forward of amidships, came the mast, after which spare spars and sweeps were stowed fore-and-aft in two vertically mounted iron hoops. Finally, the small neat companion hatch at the fore end of the snug self-draining cockpit, with its one seat athwart-ships at the after end. The big Bristol cutter *Pet* had a lavatory pan built into one corner of the cockpit seat. Behind the cockpit coaming was the main horse and rudder post.

The lower mainsheet block was not on a running traveller but was located at the centre of the horse by two very heavy flanking coil springs, or buffers. These buffers were highly necessary as the cutters were frequently gybed all standing as a standard manoeuvre when working and there was seldom time – or hands – to spare for the refinement of overhauling the sheet to ease the load. Generally speaking, the horse was about 2ft to 2ft 6in in length and was mounted between two very strong iron uprights, just high enough to allow clearance for the cranked tiller arm. In the more recent boats the tiller arm was also of iron but fitted with a turned wooden hand grip.

On the port deck, abaft the main rigging, was kept the boarding punt, in chocks and right way up. This was usually a clinker-built boat about 13ft × 5ft × 2ft 6in, often painted white so as to be easily identified at night and was used to transport the pilot to or from the ship. It was in the handling of this punt that the only real difference between the Bristol and Welsh pilots made itself apparent.

Skiffs built for Bristol men had fairly high bulwarks, of about 1ft 6in to 2ft, with a removable section through which the punt was launched and usually rowed to and from the ship, whereas the Welsh yawls had a much lower bulwark of about 1ft over which the punt was handled and sculled away with a single oar – a method which one would have thought difficult in rough water.

Many punts had a standing wire strop fastened between the inside of the stem and transom. An eye was spliced into the strop at the point of balance, and to get the punt back on board the cutter a burton from the masthead was made fast to the eye in the strop, thus making it comparatively easy to hoist her inboard.

Much has been talked and written about punts being gybed aboard with the painter made fast to the main boom, but research has proved that this was seldom, if ever, done, and certainly not if the 'boss' was on board, as misjudgement could have smashed the punt or the bulwark, or both. This would, of course, have crippled the cutter as a working unit since, with its punt out of action, the only alternative means of putting the pilot on or taking him off a ship would be in taking the cutter herself alongside, with consequent danger to her hull or top hamper in anything but a flat calm.

The only other major deck fittings not yet mentioned are the four stout samson posts, two on either side abreast the cockpit. Gun-tackle purchases to the staysail sheets were made fast to the forward pair, to which the tails of the sheets were also belayed. The after pair were used to belay the two ends of the double-ended mainsheet. (Fig 3.)

As mentioned earlier the spars were of pine and very heavy in order to eliminate as much supporting rigging as possible, as in the case of the bowsprit which, although sometimes fitted with an adjustable bobstay, was innocent of shrouds. These would have been an embarrassment on a spar which was frequently reefed or extended outboard with changes of jib.

The mainmast was a stout spar boasting shrouds but no backstays, and was usually surmounted by a short fidded topmast which was supported by a topmast forestay and a pair of wire shrouds, but often no spreaders and, again, no topmast backstays. Some of the later boats had pole masts and all had a light crane fitted at about 45 degrees to port above the hounds.

Whilst the gaff was conventional, the boom was distinguished in later craft by incorporating 'Appledore' roller-reefing gear at the gooseneck – a simple worm and wheel device by means of which the boom could be rotated, winding the mainsail around itself down to the required area in a fraction of the time it would have taken to tie reef points (Fig 4). This meant, however, that the length of the spar was limited to terminate immediately above the main horse, as obviously the main sheet pivoting band had to be located at the extreme end, thus limiting in turn the size of the mainsail.

One disadvantage of the roller-reefing method was the enormous strain put on the boom when, due to its being rolled down, the leech of the sail exerted a load on the unsupported point between gooseneck and mainsheet. And by the law of perversity, the harder it blew the nearer to the middle of the boom came the leech of the sail and the greater the strain at the weakest point. Not surprisingly therefore some broken booms resulted, but even so, the advantage of being able to reduce sail rapidly with a minimum of crew (often one man only), outweighed the disadvantage of the fairly long odds of suffering a broken boom.

Nevertheless many boats stuck to point reefing, with four sets of reef points in the main and two in the foresail. The latter remained, of course, even after the introduction of roller reefing on the main. On a point-reefing mainsail, the fourth set of points brought the gaff-jaws down almost to the boom gooseneck and in these hard-sailed craft one can imagine the desperate conditions under which this became necessary.

Below decks the lay-out in all cutters was pretty well standard (Fig 5). Once over

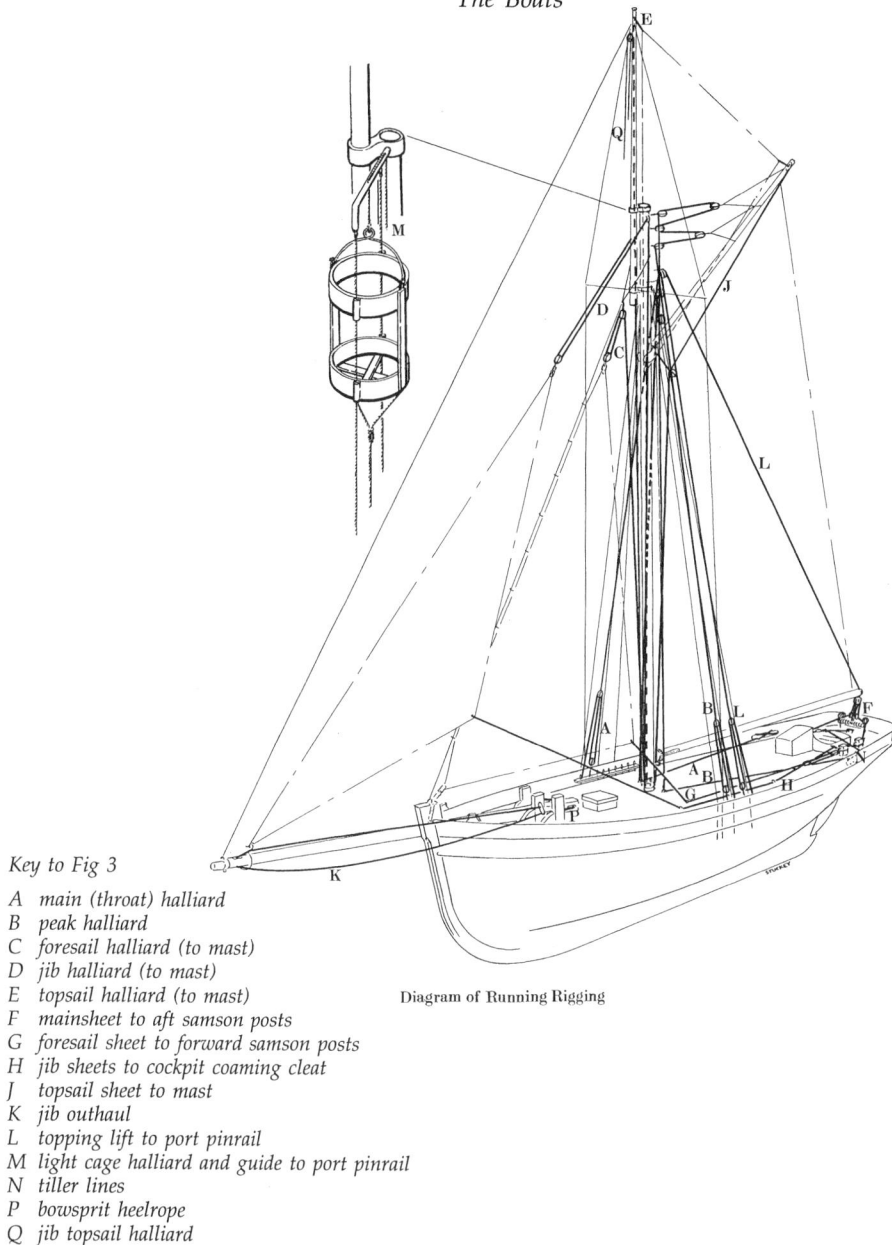

Diagram of Running Rigging

Key to Fig 3

A  main (throat) halliard
B  peak halliard
C  foresail halliard (to mast)
D  jib halliard (to mast)
E  topsail halliard (to mast)
F  mainsheet to aft samson posts
G  foresail sheet to forward samson posts
H  jib sheets to cockpit coaming cleat
J  topsail sheet to mast
K  jib outhaul
L  topping lift to port pinrail
M  light cage halliard and guide to port pinrail
N  tiller lines
P  bowsprit heelrope
Q  jib topsail halliard

*Fig 3*   Running rigging diagram of a pilot cutter

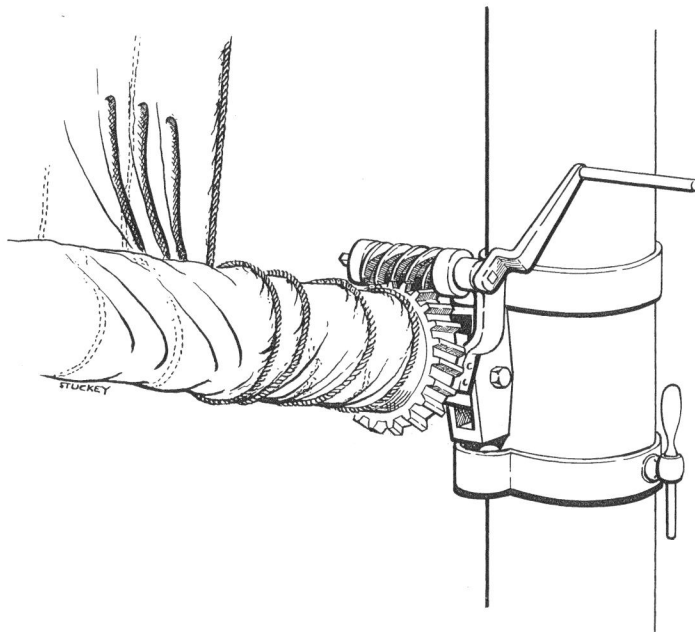

*Fig 4*   Roller-reefing gear

the high wash-board set in the lower part of the main companion hatch, one descended the companion ladder to a short passageway just forward of the quarters, or 'the runs' as this part of the vessel was called by the Newport men. On either side of the passageway were compartments for stores, oilskins, sails and other ship's gear. Some boats even boasted a wc, but this refinement was unusual as the ship's rail and open sea were considered sufficient to satisfy these requirements.

At the fore-end of the passage there was a pair of doors leading in to the main saloon. Sometimes these doors were glass panelled – as in the case of Frank Trott's *Marguerite* where the glass panels were figured in the form of the marguerite flower. Along each side of the saloon ran a settee and flush with its back, was an elliptical opening giving access to a pilot berth. This opening had sliding doors which, when closed, ensured that the occupant was not pitched out in rough conditions.

The after corners and starboard forward corner of the saloon usually contained shelves and lockers fitted with brass 'fiddles'.

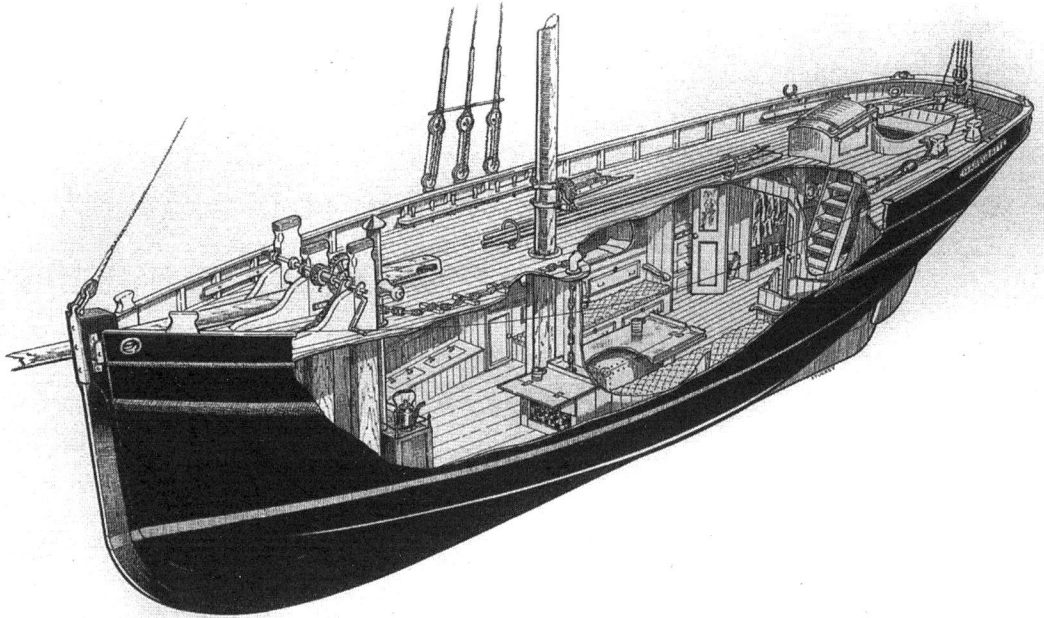

*Fig 5*

In the more sophisticated craft these corner units were sometimes quite elaborately made in polished wood and had ornate carving. To port and at the fore end of the saloon was the table, which sometimes covered a water tank – the latter being laboriously filled from a wooden cask by the apprentice whenever the cutter was in harbour.

A bulkhead divided the saloon from the forecastle which contained another water tank of about 60 gallons capacity, the chain locker, two built-in bunks for the crew, sail racks, food store and, secured against the bitt timbers, an enormous black iron coal range with black iron kettles to match. One old friend of mine relates how, in his early sea-going days as 'man-in-the-boat' to a Welsh pilot, he spent many a miserable

Pilot yawl *Stranger*, built for Thos. Richards of Cardiff by Thos. Saundry of Porthleven in 1875. Seen at Ilfracombe in the 1880s.

hour in the pitching forecastle cooking a meal for the ship's company with a bucket alongside him!

Keeping the ends of the boat light was almost a religion among the pilots and woe betide anyone who put as much as a spent match forward of the bitts or aft in the quarters. In fact, weight distribution was such a fetish with 'Slippery' Tom Williams of Cardiff in his famous old *Polly* that, when racing in the annual regattas, he shipped an anvil which he placed on a marked spot on the cabin sole.

To the pilots, the performance of their boats was of paramount importance and a constant topic of conversation along the waterfront. As regards speed on service, Grahame Farr has recorded two particularly interesting events recalled by Pilot William J. Russell, one of the Pill veterans. The first took place in the winter of 1907 when Russell was a westernman in the *Hilda*, No 2 (Enoch E. Watkins). They were in Lundy Roads, in unpleasant weather, hanging on to a tug because the wind, strong and a little to the west of south, made it impossible to anchor with safety. Cruising nearby was the *Emma*, No 20 (Edward Rowland), under four rolls of mainsail, reefed foresail and storm jib. At about 4pm they saw the *Emma* increase canvas, hoist her pilot flag and stand towards the south end of Lundy. About ten to fifteen minutes later she showed the Anglo-American private signal rocket and almost immediately the steam tanker *Potomac*, bound for Avonmouth, came into sight. Pilot Rowlands shortly afterwards boarded her and it then became too dark to see what happened.

During the night the wind increased, with heavy rain, but blew from the same direction. At 8am next morning the *Hilda* was still hanging on to her tug when they saw a skiff approaching, which proved to be the *Emma*. She hailed the *Hilda*, reefed her mainsail to five rolls, reefed her staysail and kept under way. At dinner time, to the *Hilda*'s chagrin, she boarded an Elder Dempster passenger steamer. It later transpired that between boarding the *Potomac* at about 4.30pm and being sighted at 8am, the *Emma* had sailed for home with the advantage of the tide and reached Avonmouth as the tanker was in the Old Dock locks. Pilot Rowland had rowed off and boarded her and, just as the tide began to ebb, they once more set sail for Lundy, knowing that the Elder Dempster liner was due. The tide was a neap, making no more than two or three knots, but the wind remained on the beam and strong. The distance of about 150 miles was accomplished in just over 15 hours, a speed of about 10 knots over the ground. The *Emma* was built in 1902 by Rowles and the *Hilda* in 1899 by Cooper, both at Pill.

The second incident mentioned by Pilot Russell occurred in 1911 or thereabouts. He was then a westernman in the *Freda*, No 8 (W. Selway and Samuel Buck). One morning they set out from Pill soon after the 8am train had brought the Bristol papers with their shipping intelligence. The wind was fresh and northerly and they had to beat out of the river. On clearing the mouth they were in company with the *Lily*,

The pilot cutter *Madcap*,
built by Davis & Plain,
Cardiff, in 1875 and
still sailing in 1999.
[courtesy National
Museum of Wales]

John Morgan's
*Cardiffian* with a
holiday party
aboard at Ilfracombe.
[courtesy N Alexander]

Racing cutters rounding the English and Welsh Grounds lightvessel. Jib topsails were not normally used when working.

No.19 *Spray* of Newport entering Ilfracombe Harbour in December, 1900.
[courtesy Ilfracombe Museum]

No 24 (William Hunt) and the two skiffs began to race. The wind remained in the same direction but freshened. At midnight they were off Pendeen, and Pilot Buck boarded the steamer *Nymegen*. When rounding the Land's End they were in sight of the *Lily* and again at 8am next morning when they were three miles south of the Eddystone. Sad to relate, they both missed the New Zealand steamer they were seeking. On this occasion they covered two ebbs and two floods with a strength of 3–5 knots, and the distance from Avonmouth to Plymouth being approximately 236 miles, they averaged 10 knots for the 24-hour run. The *Freda* was built in 1899 by Rowles at Pill and the *Lily* in 1905 by Bowden at Porthleven.

The various regattas at Bristol Channel ports and watering places always included races for pilot craft. One of the first skiffs to attract attention on account of her speed was the *Polly*, built by Davis & Plain at Cardiff in 1878. She carried off many trophies and doubtless caused some heartburning among the Pill fraternity. The palm was retrieved in 1893 when Rowles launched the *Marguerite* for Pilot Frank Trott of Cardiff. She had a long run of successes, including firsts at Cardiff regatta in 1895, 1896, 1897, 1905 and 1907. Happily she is still with us and her late owner has a photograph of her in racing trim showing an immense mainsail with its boom projecting 6ft outboard and a hand hanging over the counter with a syringe to keep the leach wet to stop it shaking.

It is generally acknowledged that the Bristol Channel pilot cutter was the most advanced fore-and-aft sailing craft of her time and had she been granted a few more years in commercial service it would have been interesting to see how she would have evolved. For *evolve* is the word, rather than *design*, since in common with all other small commercial sailing craft she was built, almost literally, by rule of thumb – the product of the intuition and instinct of men whose very existence relied upon keeping the seas, winter and summer, in the harsh conditions of the Bristol Channel and the Atlantic.

Douglas H.C. Birt, in the *Trident* magazine of December 1951 had some interesting comments to make on this subject, relating the form of traditional sailing craft to modern yacht design. He quoted Conor O'Brien as stating that the nearer a yacht approaches a pilot cutter or fishing boat, the safer investment she is, adding that there are no indications that fifty years of yacht designing have produced anything better. The article continued:

> Two questions seem to be involved: firstly, would cruising yachts be better today had they followed the lead of pilot cutter and fisherman rather than the racing yacht? Or, secondly, would the experience gained in yacht design have wrought such modifications in hulls and rigs of working craft that they, rather than the yachts, would have been influenced?

. . . When Harold Clayton of Penarth, a yacht designer whose work had great charm, produced a full set of drawings for the Bristol Channel pilot cutter which became the *Faith*, he had done something which nobody, it seems, had done before. And this was late in the history of these great craft. The rest had been formed by the eye of the shipwright as he built the boat. Yet the Bristol Channel pilot cutters were the most advanced of all coastal craft and built to ply a richer trade than the others. . . . We shall be forgetting half their glory unless we recall that they were built by poor men for poor men, suffering from the two great spiritual evils of poverty – ignorance and prejudice. That they still produced fine boats is to the glory of natural man, who, living close to elemental things, develops an instinct for the earth or the sea which passes sophisticated understanding.

Birt's drawings in the *Trident* show three stages in the evolution of the pilot cutter. The first, a traditional straight-stemmed, long straight-keeled type. The second, a later type similar to the design for the *Faith* but with some overhang forward, more flare in the bow section and a hollowing of the garboards with the emergence of a separate keel to give a better grip of the water and the ability to sail closer to the wind. The third sketch is based on the famous yacht *Dyarchy* by Laurent Giles, a design which represents a further refinement of the Clayton hull and which, Mr Birt suggests, would have been approaching the ultimate in pilot boat evolution. His train of reasoning is not new and the pros and cons of his argument have been and will continue to be discussed by sailing people as long as there are boats to set sail to wind. But one undeniable fact remains: the pilot cutters of the Bristol Channel did their job magnificently.

An anecdote in John Muir's book, *Messing about in Boats*, illustrates perfectly the seaman's regard for the qualities of the Bristol Channel pilot boat. Muir had purchased the Newport cutter *Maud* out of the pilot service and had engaged an old pilot-boat hand to help him take her to her new home port. During the night Muir was at the helm when the weather suddenly deteriorated. Wet through, cold and with a rapidly rising wind and a following sea, he eventually decided to heave-to, so went below to call the old man who was instantly awake in the manner of the professional seaman. On hearing Muir's reason for rousing him there was a moment's silence then he said, 'Heave-to? You don't heave-to in *them* ships unless you're waiting for something!' He then turned on his side and composed himself for sleep once more.

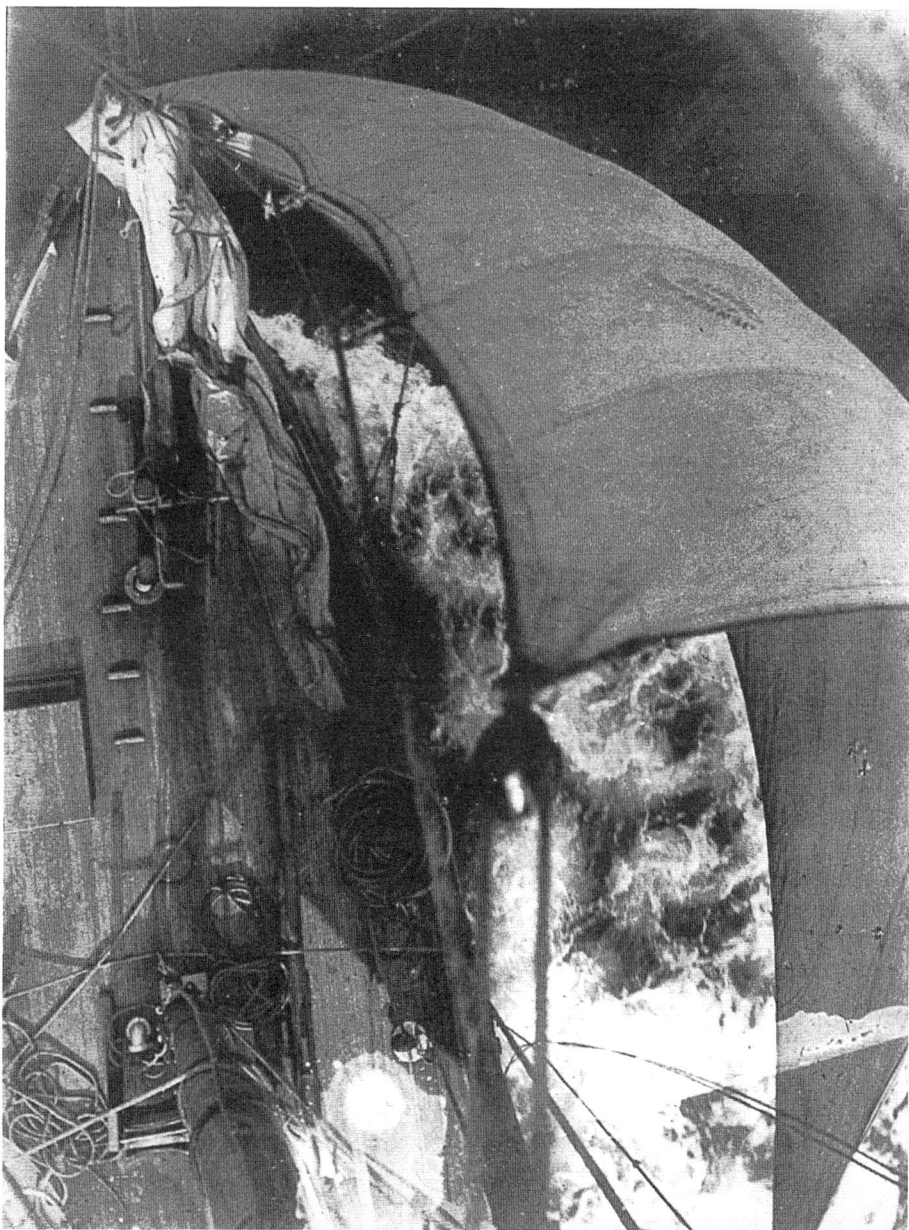

A striking view down the luff of a pilot cutter's foresail under way. Name of cutter unknown, but sail made by Jenkins of Cardiff. Note fo'c'sle stove pipe immediately abaft port bitt head, and battens on foredeck in way of anchor chain. [courtesy N Alexander]

Another impressive view from aloft, illustrating the deck layout, lead of halliards and sheets and stowage of punt. The sail in the punt is the tops'l: note headstick. [courtesy N Alexander]

# CHAPTER THREE

# The Swansea Pilot Boats

Whilst the foregoing descriptions of Bristol Channel pilot boats apply in essence to those of the majority of the pilot ports, an exception must be made in the case of Neath and Swansea whose pilot craft were quite distinctive in rig from the cutters of the rest of the Channel. These unique vessels were discussed fully in an excellent article in *The Mariner's Mirror*, entitled 'Swansea Bay Pilot Boats' by Mr J.F. Coates and I can do no better than to quote him in full, complete with illustrations and footnotes.

> The pilot boats serving the port of Swansea from the end of the eighteenth century, or even earlier,[1] carried a distinctive rig, different from any other found in the British Isles, and perhaps unique. They could be described as two-masted schooners with a considerable rake on the mainmast. The gaffs were very short, and instead of employing the usual hoops the sails were laced to the masts. From the time of its introduction the rig was kept with very little modification for over a century. It appears that it was suited to local conditions and the traffic of these boats amongst the shipping in the Mumbles Roads.
>
> The origin of the rig is obscure. Locally, the pilot boats were often spoken of as being lugger-rigged, although in appearance they would be regarded as schooners. The view most widely held by surviving pilots who served in sail, and that put forward in contemporary speeches, favours their development from the luggers found on the south-west coast in the eighteenth century. The shallop (Fig 6a, after Blankley), from which the earliest type of Swansea boat is hardly distinguishable, is described variously as 'a small light vessel, with only a small main and foremast and lug sail to haul up and let down on occasion'[2] and as 'a sort of large boat with two masts, and usually rigged like a schooner'.[3] It was quite a common rig for ships' boats over a considerable period, and following Dutch example was often used in more pretentious pleasure craft.
>
> Pictures and engravings of the harbour at Swansea and of the bay usually portray some of these two-masted boats, often to the exclusion

*Fig 6*   Swansea pilot boats

of any other type. Precisely when the shallop first made its appearance among the shore boats of Swansea Bay is not known, but by 1790 the type was very firmly established and outnumbered all others. It is remarkable that the Swansea pilots should have shown such unswerving preference for the two-masted rig over the cutter which found favour in nearly every other port in the country.

A word should first be said about the factors which governed the design of the pilot boats at Swansea. The old port in the mouth of the Tawe was formed by a short stone pier, now the landward end of the modern West Pier, and a breakwater enclosing an area to the east of the harbour known as Fabian's Bay, where now the docks are for the most part to be found. The old harbour dried out almost completely at most ebb tides and faced south-west, very nearly into the prevailing wind. It was common in the last century for the port to become packed with shipping during periods of persistent south-west winds, when all but the most weatherly craft were wind-bound. For work under such conditions the pilot boats

had to be handy little craft able to put out into Swansea Bay in most
weathers to secure the pilotage of ships running to the port for shelter.
The Mumbles Roads, four miles across the bay, where shipping could lie
off the port, did not provide very good holding ground in a wind. Thus
the services of the pilot boats at Swansea, as at many other of the more
exposed ports, were required most urgently in heavy weather and the
greatest simplicity and handiness always remained an essential requirement in their design. When putting the pilot aboard it was necessary that
the sails should be handled easily while alongside and hoisted quickly in
sheering off. This could be done without difficulty in the early 20ft boats,
but as their size and seaworthiness grew the need to keep down the
weight aloft was met by the adoption of relatively still shorter gaffs. It
would appear that the jib came into use primarily (although its
introduction at this time became widespread) in order to permit the use
of extra sail area needed to drive the heavier boats of the period 1840–60.
The use of a jib and short gaffs led to an exaggeration of the early
tendencies to maintain balance of the sail plan and resulted in a quite
distinctive rig.

Some pilot boats are depicted in a print of Swansea harbour, dated
1822. These are shown clinker-built, with no bowsprit or jib, and the
foremast is stepped in the eyes of the boat (Fig 6b). The regulations of
1791 laid down by the Harbour Trust required that 'Each pilot . . . shall
have at his command a boat of twenty-one feet stowage, six and a half
feet wide, and not less than two feet seven inches depth to the gunwale,
fitted complete with six oars for towing ships or vessels, with his name
printed thereon according to the law . . .'.[4] The gaffs, about 6ft long, are
in proportion to waterline length longer than those fitted to their
successors built around 1830 and the rake of the mainmast, though
noticeable, is not pronounced. (It is worth noting that a photograph
taken at Port Eynon, Gower, in 1879 shows a clinker-built (? crabbing)
boat masted so as to suggest shallop rig (Fig 6c) and recalling this pilot
boat of 1822 R.M.N.) Later paintings, c.1840 (see Fig 7), show a larger
craft having a heavy carvel-built hull, about 30ft long, with full bows
and a wide transom stern, although it does appear that a few had
counter sterns and that not all were entirely undecked. Both masts and
the mainboom were about as long as the waterline and the boom over-
hung the stern considerably with half its length outboard. The rake of
the mainmast, which is such a distinctive feature of the rig, would
counter the tendency of the centre of effort of each sail to shift forward
as a result of the use of short gaffs. Owing to this rake a great length of

45

*Fig 7*  Swansea pilot schooner

boom between the sheet block and boom end was necessary, since the
highest reef cringle, in being hauled down to the boom for a close reef,
moved parallel with the mast and forward nearly a third of the boom's
length. The boom became shorter in later days when the sail plan was
not so generous and the number of rows of reef points fewer.

The halliards for main and foresail were rove through two sheaves in
the masthead, one below the other, and through a single block on the
gaff, fitted about a third of the gaff's length from the throat of the sail.
The foresail halliard was secured to wooden cleats by the gunwale
abreast of the foremast, and one end was provided with a purchase
which was usually on the port side. The mainsail halliard was secured at

46

the foot of the mast so as not to foul the foresheet when close-hauled. It could be led out to the weather gunwale if the boat was being pressed in the breeze. The jib outhaul was hitched under an iron cleat on one side of the stem near the waterline and served to some extent as a bobstay when the jib was hoisted.

In other respects the arrangement of the jib was orthodox. A painting of the *Tom Rosser* in the possession of Mrs Stephen Thomas, Swansea, shows the heel of the bowsprit housed in bitts barely a foot before the fore-mast. Other details portrayed included a half-decked hull with cockpits in the stern and round the mainmast (this does not seem to have been a general feature in this type), and the usual four rows of reef points extending some 10ft up from the foot of the fore and mainsails. The mast lacing, which can be seen in most illustrations, ran through thimbles in the luff of the sails and through the four reef cringles. Its upper end was bent to the throat thimble, whence it led down to the thwart, pursuing a zigzag course around the front of the mast. Steel, in his *Mastmaking, Rigging and Sailmaking* of 1794, laces his 10-gun ship's driver boom sail in the same manner and Darcy Lever's *Young Sea Officer's Sheet Anchor* shows a similar lacing for a ship's mizzen.

In the Swansea regattas held annually until about 1900 the pilot boat races were the two main events. All the boats participated and were prepared for racing with much care, even it is said to the extent of applying to their hulls a mixture of beer and blacklead to improve the surface. To give a greater spread of sail during the racing season, larger spars were shipped, the 'summer' masts, as they were called, being about 4ft longer than those usually carried. The results of the races show that in general there was only a short interval of time separating the first and last boats. All were very similar in design and size so that the races were close contests. The last of the open boats to race was the *Swanzey*. She last appeared in the 1866 regatta but was still afloat in 1871.

The Channel Islands fishing boats had several rigging features in common with the Swansea craft. Instead of the mainsail on the raking mast, the Channel Islands' boats had, in addition to a smaller mainsail, a main topsail and a small mizzen. Both had their sails laced to the masts and the masts were of equal length. These likenesses suggest that both types developed independently along similar lines from the old two-masted square-sailed boat. Contemporary statements in the local press mention similarities to the New York pilot schooners, but a schooner rig which was roughly similar in appearance was very popular on the Atlantic seaboard of America for two centuries.

47

Pilot schooners at Swansea c.1845. [courtesy National Maritime Museum]

The South Dock (the second dock to be built at Swansea) was opened in 1859 and larger ships engaged in foreign trade were able to use the port. The competition for the pilotage of these ships caused the pilots to range far out to sea, off Lundy Island, and on occasion even as far as Land's End and Milford. The new type of boat built for this work around the sixties was much increased in size and had a hull indistinguishable in form from that of the Bristol Channel pilot cutters which are well known for their sea-keeping qualities. When in harbour the pilot boats berthed in the South Dock Half-Tide Basin near the Pilot House, whereas formerly they had to dry out at low water. This enabled the new boats to be built with a deep keel giving a draught of from 6 to 8ft, and they did not normally take the ground. When this was necessary (as for cleaning) they used legs whenever possible on account of the great rise of their floors. The rig was retained, enabling the pilots to continue to board ships directly by sailing alongside, and no standing rigging of any kind was introduced in spite of a considerable increase of mast height. Simplicity of gear continued to be essential as it was sometimes necessary to return to harbour and dock single-handed. The crew usually consisted of the master and two paid hands, so that with the three pilots there were six men aboard on the outward trip.

The appearance of the Swansea pilot boats in later years is shown in Fig 8. Like the (Welsh) Bristol Channel pilot cutters they had a low 6 or 8in rail and all had counter sterns. The deck was clear except for the usual fittings which were kept small, and they were not fitted with a winch for handling ground tackle. The mast lacing was changed to a spiral form: some photographs show either seizing with a thimble worked in it or staysail hanks connecting the luff of the sail to the lacing, but on other boats the lacing simply ran through cringles stuck in the luff of the sail. It was necessary for the lacing to run so that it could be cast off at the deck. The sail would then slack away and slide easily down the mast and no downhaul was required. The mast length on all the decked boats was 40ft, to within a foot. The expense of this heavier gear and the greater difficulty of unshipping the masts led to the abandonment of the summer rig. Nevertheless the new boats outsailed the old, since they could be driven harder and had cleaner lines. The sail plan in proportion to waterline length had become smaller. The foresail was made of slightly heavier canvas than the mainsail and the foremast became a little greater in diameter than the mainmast because the foresail was frequently used alone for running in heavy weather. The foresail halliard took the form shown in the drawing of the *Grenfell*

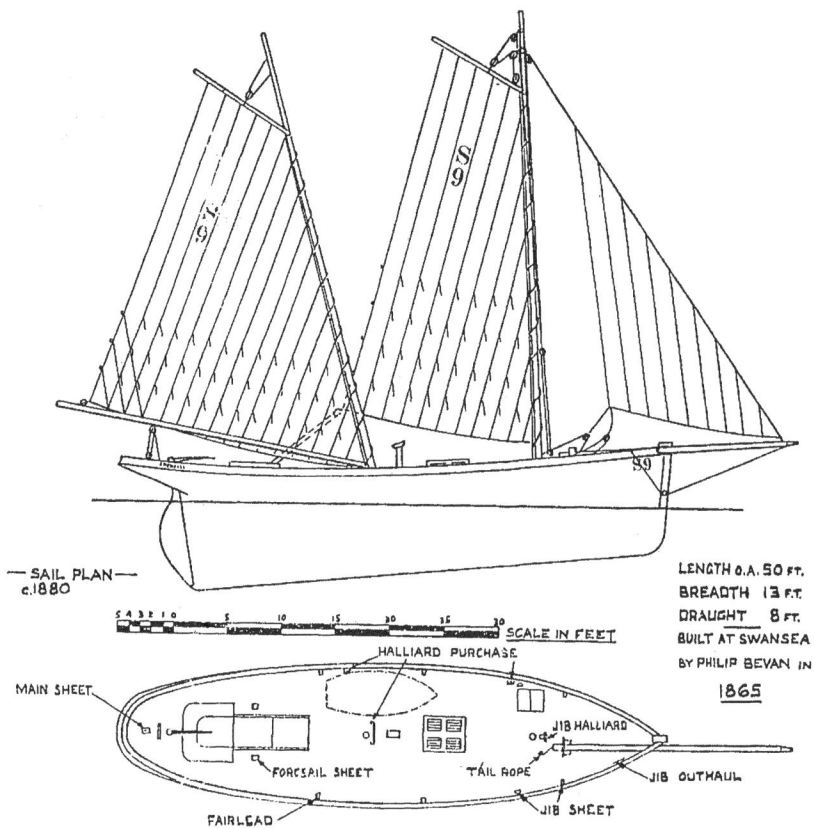

— SAIL PLAN —
c.1880

SCALE IN FEET

LENGTH O.A. 50 FT.
BREADTH 13 F.T.
DRAUGHT 8 FT.
BUILT AT SWANSEA
BY PHILIP BEVAN IN
1865

MAIN SHEET

HALLIARD PURCHASE

JIB HALLIARD

FORESAIL SHEET

TAIL ROPE

JIB OUTHAUL

FAIRLEAD

JIB SHEET

P.J.STUCKEY AFTER J.F.COATES

*Fig 8*   The Swansea pilot schooner Grenfell

(Fig 8), being of greater power to handle the heavier sail. No sheet horse was used for the mainsheet which was shackled to an eyebolt abaft the rudder head. The foresail sheets led back to points on either side of the cuddy hatch and were secured to cleats in the deck within reach of the cock-pit. The tack of the mainsail came low and the boom jaws worked on a collar just above the deck. To reduce the risk of fouling it was usual to unship the boom when the boats were berthed in harbour. At the same time the bowsprit would be run in to one side of the foremast and over the skylight, a tailrope being fitted in the inboard end for this purpose. When shipped, the bowsprit was kept in position by a bolt passed through it which bore up against the fore side of the bitts in the usual manner.

Reports of regattas at Newport and Swansea in which Swansea boats raced with Bristol Channel pilot cutters show that there was little to choose between the two types as regards speed when racing, in spite of the balloon canvas carried by the cutters. There was much local pride in being able to equal them on working sails and a big jib. In light airs, however, the cutters probably took the lead. The quality of the rig is well illustrated by an incident which occured in the 1869 Newport regatta when the *Camilla* carried away her mainmast during the race but immediately headed for Swansea, where she arrived with little delay under foresail alone.

By 1890 the Swansea copper trade had come to an end and thus most of the foreign shipping, and the conditions which had developed the large pilot boats, had disappeared. Change in the character of the trade and the institution in the eighties of definite pilotage stations off the port removed the incentive to meet ships far out to sea. Steamers required pilotage into the port at all times and it became usual for the boats to tow a 10ft punt astern for use when the wind fell light; also for use in calms and for getting in and out of harbour, 20ft sweeps were carried and worked from crutches between the masts. In the nineties the boom was shortened and the sail plan reduced (latterly the boom extended sometimes only as far as the rudder-head). Another characteristic feature of the rig was lost when some pilots replaced the mast lacing by the orthodox hoops. The reason for this reversion to usual practice is not clear today, but at the end of the nineteenth century the port was assuming its modern aspect and the pilot boats, by now nearly forty years old, were feeling their age. It should be mentioned that a cutter-rigged boat served the port for about ten years before the introduction of a steam pilot boat. She was the *Mary*, brought from the Portsmouth district to replace the *T.W.T.* which was cut down in the bay about 1885 and later transferred to Cardiff.

When the steam cutter arrived in 1898, two of the sailing craft remained in a standby capacity. They were the *Grenfell* (S9), and the *Benson* (S4), which were two of the biggest boats and in the best condition. In 1904 they, too, were disposed of, the *Grenfell* going to Bristol as a hulk or 'gadget', and the *Benson* being sold as a yacht and renamed the *Mafeking*. She was a heavy boat with an exceptionally deep draught of 11ft and a clear 6ft 6in under the beams in her cabin. As a yacht, her masts were planed down a little and lighter canvas bent, with hoops instead of lacing. A forestay with staysail was fitted and under this and a double-reefed mainsail she was a comfortable boat in most weathers. After about 1906 she was laid up for some years in the docks before eventually drifting ashore in Swansea Bay, where her timbers, now deep in the sand, are all that remain of the old fleet.

The drawing of the *Grenfell* (Fig 8) is a reconstruction showing her appearance about 1880. The sails are taken from a Swansea sailmaker's book and details of the rigging and deck fittings were either obtained from old photographs or given verbally by pilots who used the sailing boats and who are still alive today. The position of cleats and fairleads are only approximate. The halliard purchases were on the port side and, as on the earlier boats, the mainsail purchase, though normally secured to the fiferail at the foot of the mainmast, could be led out to the gunwale in a freshening wind. The hatch leading down to the forepeak is unusually high and was probably the result of a modification during service. It is unfortunate that no detailed plans have survived. At present only one model (of the *Vivian*, S1) and one contemporary sailplan are known to exist in Swansea. Reputedly drawn in 1885 by Philip Bevan, boatbuilder, the plan shows, in outline only, a very light craft with a considerable spread of canvas and lofty masts. The plan of a Swansea pilot boat (c.1870) prepared by the Coastal and River Craft Sub-Committee of the Society for Nautical Research (Fig 9) was based upon this and probably also upon a small photograph of the *Vigilant* taken in 1861. This plan therefore represents in general proportions, but not in actual dimensions, only the first three of the decked type to be built (the *Vigilant*, the *Rival* built by Bevan himself, or the *Camilla*), all of which were light boats built around 1860 and very similar in most proportions to the open craft which they were superseding. They were soon out-classed by the eight that followed, and these became progressively larger as time went on. The latter are more accurately represented by the

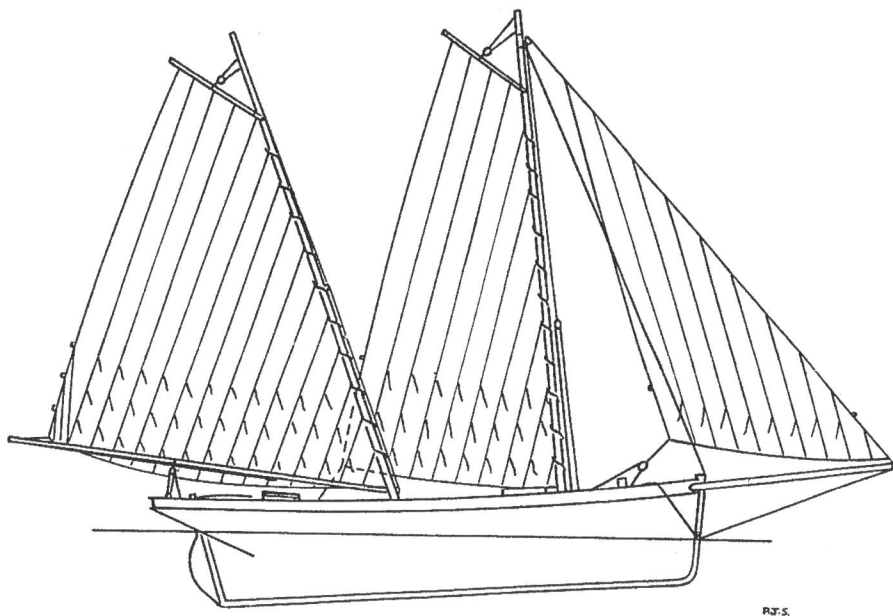

*Fig 9*   Sail plan, Swansea pilot boat c.1870

*Grenfell* (Fig 8). The drawing shows a relatively modest sailplan suited to a sea-going craft of this size.

In this short account an attempt is made to give no more than a possible explanation for the adoption of this rig by the Swansea pilots, and a very brief outline of its early development. Why it was retained for so long and how it was so well suited to local conditions are questions that cannot be answered fully from Swansea sources alone. Few records of the construction and service of these interesting craft remain and many details of build and rig have now been forgotten. Information of any kind is very incomplete, but much of that which has come to light is due to Capt J. Byrne, a retired sea pilot who was in the *Grenfell*, to Mr S.B. Davies who knew the *Benson* as a yacht, and to Messrs W.T. and T.S. Goldsworthy whose local knowledge was of great assistance. The writer desires to express his thanks to these gentlemen and especially to Mr R.

Morton Nance who not only very kindly made the drawings in this article,[5] mainly from photographs of paintings in the Royal Institution of South Wales, Swansea, and from his own sources, but also called attention to the references from Blanckley and Falconer and to some points relating to the shallop.

### Swansea pilot boats in service c. 1840–60

| No 1 | *Singleton* | No 4 | *Faith* | No 7 | *Neptune* |
|---|---|---|---|---|---|
| 2 | *Tom Rosser* | 5 | *Swanzey* | 8 | *Henry* |
| 3 | *Zion* | 6 | *Sarah* | 9 | *Providence* |
| | | 10 | *Vivian* | | |

### Decked boats in service until about 1895

| No | Name | Owner | Built | By | At | Tons | Lgth Ft | Bdth Ft |
|---|---|---|---|---|---|---|---|---|
| 1 | *Vivian* | D. Owen | 1863 | Bevan | Swansea | 22.39 | 45.6 | 11.3 |
| 2 | *Vigilant* | W. Rosser | 1859 | Bowen | Swansea | 17.12 | 41.6 | 10.9 |
| 3 | *Rival* | J. Rosser | 1861 | Bevan | Swansea | 21.15 | 43.0 | 11.6 |
| 4 | *Benson* | J. Rosser | 1870 | Bowen | Swansea | 28.27 | 51.0 | 13.6 |
| 5 | *Lizzie* | — | 1875 | Bowen (or Cocks, Bideford) | Swansea | 33.13 | 52.0 | 13.0 |
| 6 | *Glance* | W. Rosser | 1863 | Perkins | Bideford | 21.77 | 46.0 | 11.6 |
| 7 | *Alarm* | —— | 1860 | Bowen | Swansea | 19.43 | 42.0 | 11.0 |
| 8 | *T.W.T.* | G. Fox | 1863 | Bowen (or Perkins, Bideford) | Swansea | 26.16 | 48.0 | 11.6 |
| 9 | *Grenfell* | Burton | 1865 | Bevan | Swansea | 29.29 | 50.0 | 13.0 |
| 10 | *Camilla* | T. Brown | 1860 | Bowen | Swansea | 18.70 | 45.6 | 10.0 |
| 11 | *Charles Bath* | Bibby | 1865 | Cocks | Bideford | 19.00 | 49.6 | 12.0 |

*The tonnages and dimensions given here are by courtesy of the late Mr A.G. Moffat, Swansea.*

### NOTES

1. W.H. Jones, in his book, *The History of the Port of Swansea* (Carmarthen: W. Spurrell & Son, 1922), states on p.295 that the first pilot was registered as such in 1791. On the same page is to be found a very brief account of pilotage to the port which is concerned for the most part with bye-laws and the commercial aspect. No mention is made of the construction of the boats employed.

2. *A Naval Expositor*, by Thomas Riley Blanckley (1750), p.149. The illustration shows the 'lugsails' are boomless gaff sails; no jib is carried. Dutch pictures at least a century earlier show the same rig. It probably originated as an adaptation of the admired *chaloup biscalenne* in which fore-and-aft sails replaced square sails, just as true lug sails did later in the bisquines of Normandy and north-east Brittany. R.M.N.

3.  *An Universal Dictionary of the Marine*, by William Falconer (first published 1769, reprinted by David & Charles (Publishers) Ltd, Newton Abbot, 1970).
4.  This is one of the sixteen rules 'for the better regulation and government of pilots, pilot boats, hobblers and helpers of ships and vessels pursuant to an Act . . .' of 1791, which are given in *The Swansea Guide* of 1802.
5.  The drawings reproduced in this chapter were drawn by P.J. Stuckey and based upon those by Mr R. Morton Nance. Fig 8, the *Grenfell* is based upon the original drawing by Mr J.F. Coates and Fig 9 upon a drawing prepared by the Coastal and River Craft Sub-Committee of the Society for Nautical Research.

CHAPTER FOUR

# How the Boats were Built

It was the usual practice for the pilot boats to be built from a half-model which was whittled away until it satisfied the particular requirements of the pilot – and one can imagine the lengthy deliberations and head-wagging that went on over it between the pilot and his self-appointed advisors. This procedure was typical of all small commercial sailing-craft – a process of evolution rather than of design – and was applied similarly to the actual process of construction.

The half-model having been agreed upon, it was marked in sections and from these it was possible to draw out full-size patterns of the frames on the floor of the loft. As there was no external ballast the keel was massive – that of the Rowles-built *Cariad* being fairly typical at 42ft × 8in. The stem and stern posts were tenoned into the keel, which was allowed to project at the after end to provide the lower pintle for the rudder. Massive grown oak knees supported the stem and stern posts which, with the keel, provided the backbone of the assembly. A horn timber, notched into the stern post to carry the framing of the overhanging counter, was supported and strengthened by cheek pieces, one on either side, where it joined the stern post. The counter was rebated and notched to receive the shelves and bulwark stanchions as well as the planking. Trennails, or wooden dowels of about ⅝in. diameter were used as fastening for the futtocks. These were usually of oak and after they had been driven right through the prepared hole, small oak wedges were driven into the end grain of the trennails. The floors, notched and drift-bolted over the keel, were about 4in thick, about the same as the timbers which were then fixed to the sides of the floors by trennails and some clench fastening.

Spaced about 16in to 18in apart, the frames were doubled up about 8ft from both stem and stern posts. The rudder trunk – a watertight box which contained the rudder stock – extended up between the horn timber cheek pieces and was made up of four oak staves shaped on the inside to form a cylinder and keyed together by four tongues.

The hull timbers, which can be compared to the ribs of the human frame, were shaped from the half-model and then made up in the mould loft in pieces of thin wood, only half the full shape being necessary. These thin wood templates were then transferred to the uncut timbers and used as patterns, so that they could be sawn to shape. Where the curve was complex or double, the timbers would be made up of two futtocks to avoid short grain, but in any case the midship timbers were always doubled and the curves could be worked in with staggered futtocks.

The greatest difficulty with this type of construction was probably in the working of the bevels on the saw frames. These had to be exactly right, changing as they did from top to bottom on most timbers, and had to be cut on the bench from angles obtained from the lofted lines. The beam shelves, in something like 9 × 3in pitch-pine, ran fore and aft inside the frames and gave the first indication of the sheer. It was not easy – indeed sometimes impossible – to steam such members in situ on the timbers, so the usual practice was to make a rough jig or bending form, using patterns of double curvature again taken from the lofted lines. The shelves were then steamed and cramped on to the jigs before being offered up to the timbers, which were notched and to which the shelves were secured by two staggered bolts per frame, as were the stringers. In a similar manner the stringers, some 7in × 2½in, were formed before being bolted to the inside of the timbers. Two of these stringers ran fore and aft, on the bilge and under the beam shelf. The deck beams were half dove-tailed into the shelves and completed the framework.

During this initial stage of construction all the timbers were being held in position by temporary ribands running fore and aft. The timbers were also steadied by shores located in the ground or into the beams of the building shed.

It should be remembered that, except in the later craft, glues were unknown, hence the very heavy and solid construction. No comparison can therefore be made with modern boat-building methods where powerful marine glues are extensively used.

Planking was started at the sheer strake in the manner usual for all carvel hulls; then the elm garboard strake, of 24in × 1½in. section, was fitted. Its shape was taken off the framework by what was known as a 'spiling batten', then transferred to the garboard plank by means of dividers. The final fitting was carried out by trial and error, but not until limber holes had been cut in the base of the timbers to allow the flow of bilge water. The last plank fitted on the bilge was known as the shutter and its fitting was celebrated by all hands with great rejoicing.

Caulking bevels were then planed along the strakes and the plank rabbet coated with bitumen. After steaming, the strake could be fitted and secured with dumb and through rivets, all those below the waterline being bronze in many boats. Next, the sheer strakes of oak were fitted and fastened in a similar manner. The bilge strakes were all of elm and about 6in wide. The wider planks were sometimes hollowed on the inside to fit the shape of the timbers.

After the planking was completed, the outside of the hull was planed fair and the prepared seams caulked with cotton or oakum. Where the deck beams held the mast partners, lodging and hanging knees were placed, these being of oak 2½in thick and carefully bevelled to provide a tight fit. They were all riveted in position through deck beams and timbers. The pitch-pine bitt timbers were securely fastened to the floors and notched into the deck beams.

As in most work-a-day fore-and-afters, the pitch-pine deck planks were laid parallel to the king plank and not 'swept' as in a yacht. They were planed and cut with caulking seams on their upper edges and fitted tightly to the covering board. The planks were secured to the deck beams by square boat nails, the heads of which were sunk and the hole filled with a wooden plug, bedded in white lead, and with the grain running with that of the plank.

The bulwark stanchions were let through the covering board for about 18in and spiked to a timber. As previously mentioned, the height above the deck depended very largely on whether the vessel was being built for a Welsh or an English pilot, but the basic construction was the same except for the small detail of the two D-sectioned metal strips, in way of the punt's launching position, which capped the rail of a Welsh boat, whilst a Bristol skiff had a removable section in her bulwark.

Waterways were cut in the lowest bulwark strake to free the decks of water. On the starboard side of the stem post a hole was cut for the reefing bowsprit and to port was the anchor chain hawse-hole. In the average boat, cabin joinery was often of varnished tongued and grooved pitch-pine boards, although in some, such as *Marguerite*, it was more elaborate, with polished mahogany or teak.

The self-draining cockpit was often fitted with a teak coaming and most of the deck joinery was in teak. The Bristol skiff *Pet* even included a commode built into the cockpit seat! The cockpit self-draining outlets had leather flaps fastened over them against the hull, providing a 'non-return' exit for surplus water.

The only two boats known to depart from the usual practice of entirely internal ballast were the *Faith* of Barry and the *Bear* of Bristol. *Faith* was, in fact, revolutionary in several respects, having been first designed on paper, prior to forming the half-model, and incorporating a cutaway forefoot and a separate stateroom for the owner.

The following detailed specification of a typical pilot cutter of her day, that of the *Kindly Light* submitted to Pilot Lewis Alexander of Barry, is of particular interest as this fine example of her class has been preserved.

February 17th 1911

SPECIFICATION FOR A WOOD-BUILT PILOT CUTTER

*General Dimensions*: 52ft overall, 14½ft. beam, about 8½ft. draught. Length of keel, 38ft. Vessel to be built with round forefoot and elliptic stern. Cabin to be fitted with 2 berths and usual lockers. Forecastle fitted with 2 berths, lockers and racks for sails. Materials to be the best of their respective description and to be fitted in a workmanlike manner.

*Keel*: To be of English elm.

*Stem & Stern Posts*: Of English oak. Also floors, frames, stanchions and beams of oak. Knees at beams one fore and aft of mast beam.

*Keelson*: Of pitch pine.

*Planking*: 1 oak plank round top, pitch pine to bilge, stout elm bilge 2½in, remainder of plank of elm or pitch pine 1½in.

*Rails*: To be of elm or oak with greenheart capping.

*Decks*: Best yellow pine.

*Fastenings*: To be galvanized iron.

*Cabin*: To be of pitch pine and teak finish.

*Ceiling*: To be from stringer to floor of lockers.

*Bulkheads*: To be placed as required entrance from cockpit to cabin and cabin to forecastle. Cabin to have set of drawers each side of entrance from oak cockpit, curtain rail & mirror. Cockpit entrance to over beam, after companion and fore companion to be of teak. Companion and cockpit to be fastened with copper.

*Masts*: To be cutter-rigged with pole size as required. Bowsprit, boom, gaff, topsail yard, two oars, boat hook. Booming out spar.

*Ironwork on Keel*: Ballast iron.

*Ironwork on deck*: To be galvanized, three chain plates each side, all eyebolts and ironwork necessary for spars to be galvanized, head of bolts to be bevelled. Ironwork on keel to be 1in thick.

*Rigging*: Three shrouds each side of 2in wire, forestay 3½in wire running tackle. Blocks to be internal iron bound, running gear white manilla.

*Anchor*: 45 fathoms of chain galvanized; 45 fathoms of hawser and winch windlass.

*Pump*: Tube to be of copper, fitted fore side of cockpit.

*Sails*: One mainsail, one foresail, two topsails, three jibs, one balloon foresail, one spinnaker.

*Painting*: Vessel to be scraped, cemented and concreted up to bilge, to have two coats oil paint, two coats paint on bottom and top sides. Cabin to be varnished, forecastle to be grained. Brasses for rudder head and collar for trunk and head of stern post.

*Sundries and Utensils*: Four plates, four mugs, cooking stove, knives, forks and spoons, saucepans etc. Foghorn, bulb flashlight, Morse lamp, combination lamp, water tank 60 gallons, table in forecastle.

# Sails and Sailmakers

The performance of any purely sailing vessel is as dependent upon the cut and set of her sails as upon the shape of her hull and the Bristol Channel pilot craft were no exception in this respect. Indeed, unlike most commercial sailing vessels which, once loaded with a cargo, had thereby secured their job, or the sporting yachtsman to whom a lost race meant merely disappointment, the pilot put to sea to race in deadly earnest, for his very livelihood depended upon his winning.

It has already been mentioned that the mainsail was of cotton in summer and flax in winter. The winter mainsail was smaller than that used in summer but, prior to the introduction of roller reefing, both carried four sets of reef points and were loose-footed. Those used with roller-reefing were laced to a wooden jackstay or 'combe' along the boom.

The number of headsails carried depended largely on the affluence and enthusiasm of the owner, but in all boats it was usual to have a working foresail, which had two sets of reef-points, a balloon foresail and three jibs, namely the large jib or 'spinnaker', working or 'slave' jib and storm or 'spitfire' jib. A working topsail was also used, being usually a fairly small sail appropriate to the short topmast. Some were of the 'leg-o'-mutton' or peak-headed type, while others with a short head-stick were known as being 'square-headed'. In light weather a large jackyard topsail was sometimes used. The topsail was usually set to starboard.

It was not usual for the pilots to tan or 'cutch' their sails as it was essential that their number or port initial should stand out clearly, but one Welsh pilot did carry a tanned jackyard topsail for reasons of strategy. According to Captain 'Billy' Prethero, a retired pilot of Barry who served his time in the sailing cutters, his boss when 'seeking' down off the Cornish coast would sometimes cruise among the then numerous tan-sailed fishing craft, set his tanned topsail to disguise himself as one of them, and work out to the westward of a rival cutter when a ship was due – resetting his normal sail when the advantage had been gained.

In the days of working sail every port had its sailmakers and in 1896 there were about thirty journeyman sailmakers in Cardiff, according to P. Ward, a sailmaker, who wrote a short article on sailmaking for a local Cardiff journal at that time. In it he says that the work of sailmaking was carried on in about eight sail lofts, but that the 'golden age' of sailmaking in Cardiff was from 1866 to 1876 when the building of all kinds of sailing vessels reached its peak.

The principal sailmakers in Cardiff at the turn of the century were Jenkin Jones, Hambly, Davis & Plain and P. Ward, whilst in Bristol they were Dallin, Williams, Hiatt, Lambey and Tratman, some of whom were not only master sailmakers but also ship-chandlers. Occasionally a pilot would go as far as Appledore to order sails from the firm of Harris, but usually they patronised their local sailmakers. Sometimes the pilots made their own sails which is not altogether surprising as the majority had served in deep-water sailing ships during their required 'sea-time' and had learned at least the rudiments of sailmaking.

Of the Bristol sailmakers, both Dallins and Tratmans were well established by the early nineteenth century and were still in business in the 1970s, although Dallins (now absorbed into another company) ceased to make sails some time in the 1960s and turned their attention to tents, awnings and suchlike.

The following extracts from the day-book of Messrs Dallin Brothers, commencing January 1855, make interesting reading and give a good idea of the sailmaking costs incurred by a typical pilot cutter of the period. They will bring a wistful look to the eye of many a present-day yachtsman.

## Extracts from Day-Book of Dallin Bros. & Son, Sailmakers, Bristol

*1857*
Sept.    Pill Skiffs, Capt W. Reed
        New Stayforesail, 43 yds                  £3. 8. 1

Oct.    Pill Skiffs, Capt. G. Reed
        New Mainsail, 190 yds. No 2 Long Flax
        Canvas, Fixing 3 Bullseyes & galvanised
        thimble in head                      £14.10. 6

*1860*
April    (Pilot No 36) Wm. Reed
        Man to work on Mains'l, roping round and
        fixing mains'l at Pill                 8. 0
        Roping & serving twine           2. 0
                                        10. 0

May     Wm. Reed (Pilot No 36)
        2 yds wide Red Bunting           1. 8
        2 yds wide White Bunting        1. 8
                                         3. 4

Oct     Wm. George Reed
        New Mains'l 184 yds. No 2      £14.11. 4
        Fixing Bullseyes, new thimbles etc      4. 0
                                     £14.15. 4

| | | |
|---|---|---:|
| *1861* | | |
| April | Wm. Reed | |
| | New Gafftopsail 36 yds best long flax No 5 canvas | £2.14. 0 |
| July | Wm. Roland. New Mains'l 82 yds Best Long flax No 3 | 6. 9 |
| | Wm. Reed. 6yds No 2 Boiled Canvas | 6. 0 |
| | 2yds Red Bunting | 1. 8 |
| | 2 balls tar twine | 2. 3 |
| | | 9.11 |
| Aug. | Wm. Reed. 8 yds No 3 Navy Canvas | 8. 0 |
| | Repairing Mains'l at Pill, labour & twine | 5. 0 |
| | | 13. 0 |
| *1862* | | |
| May | Edwd. Canniford. Labour on Sails on Pill 13/4 days | 6. 2 |
| | Twine | 9 |
| | | 6.11 |
| Oct | J. Payne. New Mains'l 144 yds Best double wt. No 2 canvas (Stephens) | £14. 2. 0 |
| | Fixing with Bullseyes & thimbles | 6. 6 |
| | | £14. 8. 6 |
| *1863* | | |
| Dec. | Wm. Bailey. New Stays'l 45 yds No 2 | £4.13. 9 |
| *1864* | | |
| May | Wm. Gilmore. New Big Jib 86 yds Long Flax No 7 Canvas | £6.19. 9 |
| | Stay Rope 15 lb | 7. 6 |
| | | £7. 7. 3 |
| *1864* | | |
| May | Wm. Gilmore. New Big Jib 86 yds Long Flax No 7 Canvas | £6.19. 9 |
| | Stay Rope 15 lb | 7. 6 |
| | | £7. 7. 3 |
| *1864* | | |
| July | John Gilmore. New Mainsail 165 yds best Dbl. Tak. Long Flax No 2 canvas | £15.16. 3 |

| | | |
|---|---|---|
| Sept. | Alfred Ray. Repairing Mains'l, roping | |
| | leech & clew | 3. 0 |
| | Canby, 'True Blue' (No 4) | |
| | 14 yds No 3 Best repairing canvas | 18. 1 |
| Dec. | Wm. Ray. New Mains'l 167 yds Best Extra | |
| | No 2 canvas | £16.14. 0 |
| *1865* | | |
| March | Wm. Bailey. New Trys'l Jib 15 yds No 2 | |
| | Long Flax Canvas | £1. 7. 6 |
| | Stay rope & fixing | 7. 6 |
| | | £1.15. 0 |
| Sept | Charles Porter (No 6) | |
| | Mains'l 114 yds No 2 Stephens Best | £10.18. 6 |
| | Stay fores'l, Stephens Best | £2.15. 7 |
| | | £13.14. 1 |

It will be noted that the sailcloth, under the general term of 'canvas', is often graded in the customary way, by number from 1 to 6 – the lower the number the heavier the canvas. The flax cloth was manufactured in bolts, or rolls, about 40 yds long by 24 ins wide whereas the cotton came in bolts of up to 100 yds in length by 22 ins in width. Much of this material came from Scotland, but some came from the west of England.

Although sails for the pilot craft were made in exactly the same way as those for any other commercial vesels, a brief description of the procedure may be of interest. A master sailmaker or foreman did the actual cutting, but the making and sewing was divided between the hands. When the cloths had been cut and numbered, they were sewn together and the roping then added, together with reef-points, cringles etc. The rope was usually of hemp or manilla, though flexible steel was sometimes called for.

In those days of hand-sewn sails the sailmaker's equipment was simple, consisting of a low wooden bench some 7 ft long and 15 ins high, a range of needles and a sail-palm – a strap of hide which fitted around the hand and included a thumb-hole. Positioned to coincide with the operator's palm was let in a flat metal disc, indented to admit the head of a needle. Thus the sailmaker held the needle between finger and thumb with the head located in the disc thimble. He would then pierce the material with the needle and push it through, opening the hand during the last stage of penetration and using the powerful thrust of the hand and forearm muscles. Work on the lower numbers of canvas must have called for considerable stamina. A sailmaker was also expected to be competent with ropework and used a fid for splicing and

Sid Hunt of Pill, Rowles' last
apprentice.

Cooper's dry dock at Pill c.1885.
The skiff is a Gloucester/Sharpness
boat with the distinctive white
bulwark. Mr Cooper is the bearded
figure in the foreground.

seizing. He was also expected to carry out repair work on sails in situ, as can be seen from the extracts from the Dallins day-book.

As can be seen from the photographs reproduced in these pages, the cut and set of some pilot-boats sails would hardly satisfy an America's Cup skipper, but it should be remembered that many were port pilots who only worked the 'roads', being unlicensed for the Channel. Often, too, they took over old cutters whose sails and gear had to be made to last as long as possible, and it is conceivable that they sometimes utilised sails not originally made for their particular craft. As a general rule, however, the pilots took the cut of their sails very seriously indeed.

# The Builders

As Pill has always been part of the port of Bristol and a vessel's registration certificate required only the port of registry, it is probable that many craft registered as having been built in Bristol were, in fact, built at Pill. The builders of Pill whose names can be traced are: James Phillips, who built his own skiff, the *James*, in 1809; William Morgan, building 1822–40; Thomas Price, who had been building fishing and other small craft at Weston-super-Mare and came to build at Pill from 1854 to 1858; Hillhouse of Bristol also built several early skiffs, including the *Charlotte* in 1808; and William Patterson built seven skiffs in 1851. Six of those were sister vessels 43ft 3in in length and varying from 25 to 26 tons, while the seventh, of 28 tons, was 46ft 6in overall. Then there was Edwin Rowles who, starting as a shipwright in Bristol in 1877, began building at Pill in 1887. He was the last commercial builder there and his business closed down in 1910. Another was Charles Cooper who began building about 1862 and died in 1879. He left his yard to George Cooper, who was at that time building in Penarth, but he returned it to his younger brother, John Cooper, who worked in Charles's yard. John worked the yard at Pill until it closed down in 1905. Most of these builders launched small coasters of various types such as sloops, scows or schooners, and in later years fishing craft and yachts.

Of the two Pill yards which existed within the twentieth century, Coopers lay at the head of the creek, just in the shadow of the railway viaduct, and included a small dry-dock which was incorporated about 1885. Cooper was also the only builder at Pill to have his own saw-pit.

Rowles' yard was situated on the up-river side of the creek, near its mouth and close to the watch-house. His slip was just inside the creek and was overlooked by his red-brick house. His last apprentice, Sid Hunt, who survived into the 1970s, remembered how particular were the pilots when taking delivery of a new skiff and that on one occasion a pilot refused to accept a boat because he noticed that one plank was in two lengths instead of one continous run. He insisted on another plank being fitted, 'but',

Hunt recalled with a grin, 'it had to be a length of foreign wood and always gave trouble afterwards'. On another occasion an odd iron fastening in a copper-fastened boat had been used to pull in a particularly stubborn plank – one fastening among hundreds – yet the pilot, having discovered it when dried out at Ilfracombe after his first trip, came back to the yard furiously demanding an explanation.

The shipwrights on the yard were all master men, capable of working without supervision and demanding nothing less than perfection in the work of their assistants and apprentices.

An apprentice's weekly wage at the turn of the century was three shillings and sixpence for the first year, four shillings and sixpence for the second, and then an extra one shilling for every remaining year of his apprenticeship. His hours of work were 6am to 5pm with a half-hour break for breakfast and one hour for lunch.

Until the upheaval of 1861, when the Welsh and Gloucester pilot services gained their independence, the range of the pilots was restricted to Lundy Island, but after that date competition increased rapidly and the era of long-distance 'seeking' began, bringing with it the need for larger and faster boats (Fig 10). This, in turn, led to an upsurge of building by yards other than the traditional ones in the Upper Bristol Channel. Pilots went to builders as far apart as Hamble, Porthleven and Fleetwood in their quest for craft of specific qualities, spurred on by the need to keep the seas to the westward in all weathers and seasons.

Some cutters were built at Bideford and Appledore, and these were always referred to as having come from 'over the Bar'. Of those built at Bideford there were the *Lassie* of 1865 by J. Cove and the *Morning Star* of 1869 by Johnson. A later example was the well-known *Frolic* in 1905, built by Westacott Claverhouses. Like the *Faith*, the *Frolic* was of unusual design, with a peculiar cut-away several feet back from the shallow forefoot. She also had steeply cambered decks which were not popular at sea. In her later days as a cutter (she is now rigged as a schooner yacht), she was owned by Frank Trott and carried a hollow steel main boom – a very advanced innovation. The only cutter traced as having been built at Appledore was the *Village Belle* in 1887, although it is believed that another, the *Primrose*, was also built there.

Oddly enough, the famous yard of Hinks of Appledore, which has been building sailing craft for 200 years, never built a Bristol Channel pilot cutter but often repaired and refitted them.

Sometimes cutters were built in batches, as at Padstow by R. and T. Treadwell who, in 1851, built two together, and at Pill by Patterson who built the batch of seven already mentioned. Other well-known builders in the Bristol Channel were: Phillips of Cardiff, founded in 1862, who built the first Cardiff cutter; Davis and Plain, 1872; Downs, 1870; Baker and Hambly, 1890. At Penarth, cutters were built by Charles Cooper, 1863; the Penarth Yacht Building Co, 1890 (who built the *Faith* in 1904); A. Anderson, 1910, who built the *Nocomis*, as late as 1914, while at Newport could be

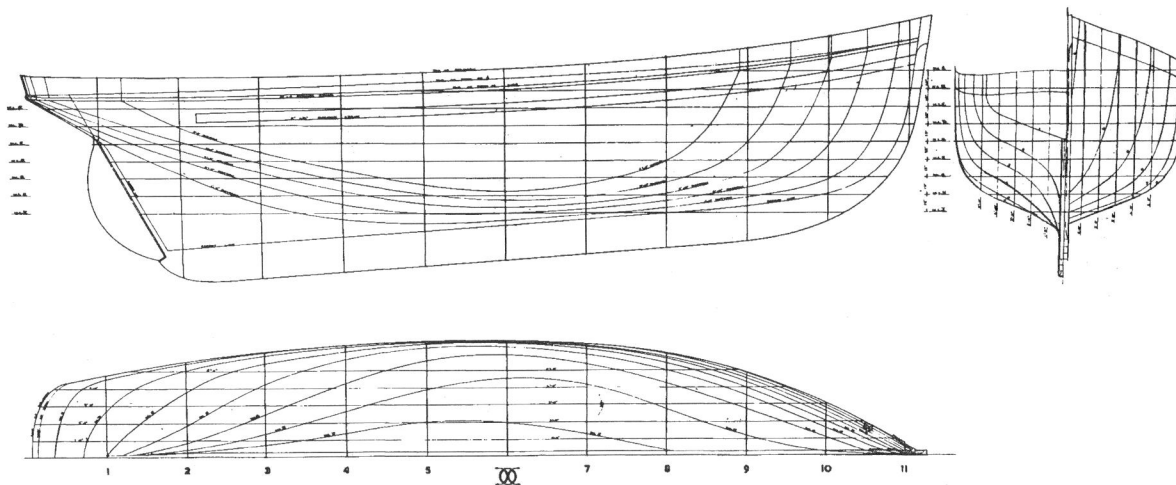

*Fig 10a*   Lines plan of the *Marguerite*, built at Pill, 1893

HERGA

BUILT COOPERS BRISTOL 1902

| L.O.A. | 47' 10" |
| L.W.L. | 40' 0" |
| DRAUGHT | 7'·2" |
| BEAM | 13' 5" |

26 TONS T.M

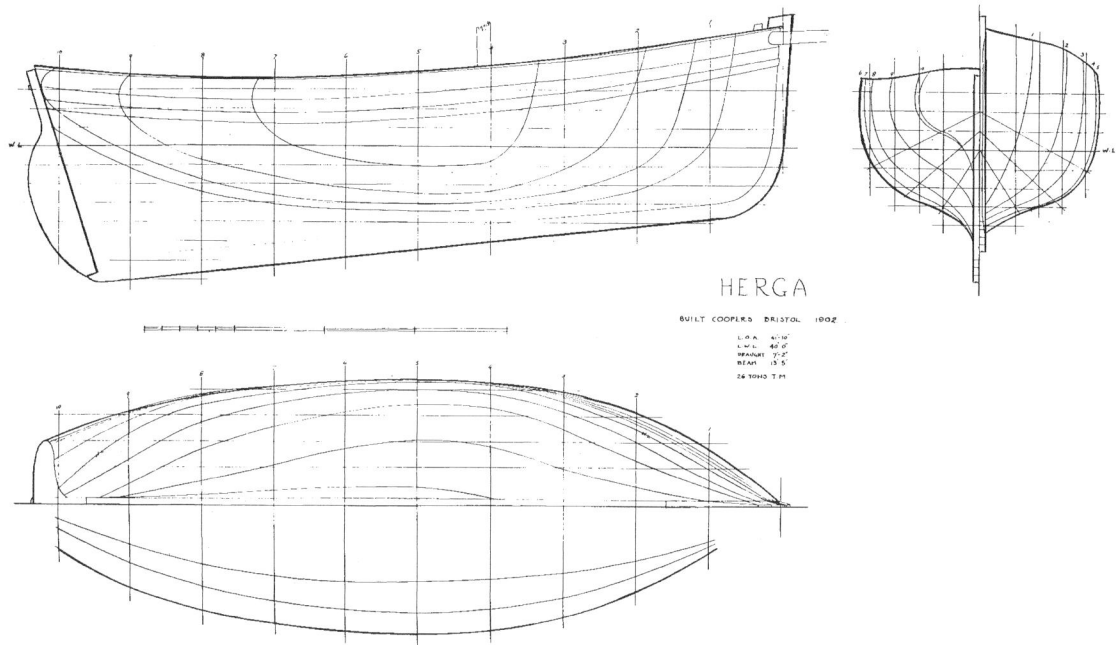

*Fig 10b*   The lines of the *Herga*, built at Bristol, 1902

Gloucester/Sharpness cutter *Alaska*, sister ship to the *Berkeley Castle*, both of which were built by Bob Davies in the 1880s. [courtesy W. Groves]

Gloucester/Sharpness cutter *Berkeley Castle* as depot ship at Portishead. She was sister ship to the *Alaska*. Both were built by Bob Davies at Saul in the 1880s.

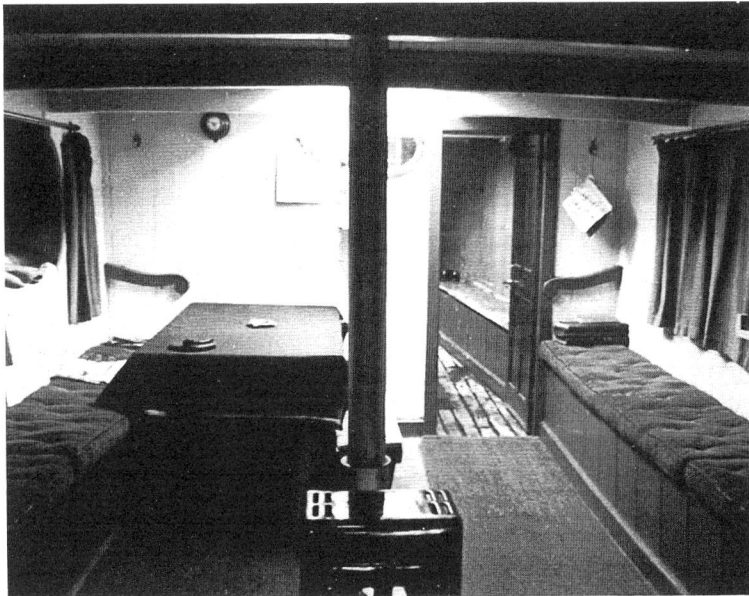

The saloon of a pilot cutter, typical except for the stove and portable radio.

The fo'c'sle stove which was usually secured to the bitt timbers.

found John Williams, 1868; William Williams, 1871; Maudie & Corney, 1876; and T. Cox who built the *Mascotte* in 1904.

The big cutters *Berkeley Castle* and *Alaska* were built for the Gloucester-Sharpness pilots in the 1880s at Saul by Bob Davis and it is said that both keels were cut from the same tree, donated by the Earl of Berkeley. They were launched sideways, due to the restricted width of the canal. The *Berkeley Castle* was reputed to be the largest pilot cutter in the Bristol Channel. At Gloucester in 1859 was the yard of another Cooper; Jeans & Levison in 1876, and W.H. Halford who built *The Solway* in 1900.

Yards outside the Bristol Channel included those of Slades at Fowey, who built the *Cornubia* in 1911; J. Bowden at Porthleven, who built the *Seabreeze* in 1899 and the *Olga* in 1909, and Kitto & Sons, also of Porthleven, who produced the *Rene B* for Pilot Bennett of Cardiff. At Hamble, Luke built the *Active* in 1883. J. Angear of Looe built the *Saladin* in 1907, while at the other end of the country, at Fleetwood, Liver & Wilding built the *Alpha* in 1904, which later prompted Lewis Alexander of Barry to go to the Fleetwood yard of Armour Brothers in 1911 for his *Kindly Light*. Both the *Alpha* and the *Kindly Light* were atypical in hull form for Bristol Channel pilot craft. Based on the lines of Lancashire shrimpers – straight-stemmed and with a low freeboard aft – they were typical fishing boats, their shallow forefoot and deep heel giving them a good performance in light conditions.

In fact, during the days when the pilot fleet could be numbered in three figures many fishing craft and yachts were converted for pilotage use and one such boat, the *Hero*, built at Ilfracombe as a fishing boat in 1888, was converted by Rowles of Pill for a Barry pilot about 1900. The Barry cutter, the *White Heather*, was said to have been built as a Cornish fishing lugger and the photograph would seem to bear this out.

It is high tribute to their builders that many of the cutters mentioned above are still in active commission as yachts and attract admiring attention wherever they go – and that can be, and often is, anywhere in the world. None of them can be less than seventy years old and one, the *Madcap*, built in 1875, still looked as smart in the 1990s as ever she did in the 1870s – a durable memento of the skill and craftsmanship of Davis & Plain of the Cardiff yard of yesteryear.

The boats were constantly at sea winter and summer and consequently needed regular maintenance in order to serve the pilots reliably and safely, so it is of interest to know what was involved in a typical major overhaul and how much it cost.

I am indebted therefore to Cornish marine historian, Tony Pawlyn, for his permission to reproduce in the following pages an entry in the ledgers of H. N. Peake, shipwright of Newlyn, a tender for the overhaul of the Newport pilot yawl *Flora*, dated 17 August 1905. It also gives a very good indication of the workforce and time involved.

### Ledgers (page 67) H. N. Peake – Shipwrights Newlyn

## Mr. J. Jones, Newport
## Tender for 'Flora'

To repair & thoroughly overhaul Pilot Boat Flora of Newport –
  Putting three New Floors & Futtocks. Six shifts of plank on
Starboard Bottom. Breaking Butts in proper order P. Pine.
  To scarf Keel & stem
  To caulk the ship from Keel to covering Board & Deck where
required & Pitched throughout.
  To refit the Interior of Ship with all Necessary Bulkhead ceiling
Risers, seats, Lockers, Bed-Berths &c.
  All Face Work of Cabin to be of P. Pine sized & Varnish.
  To make & Fit companion of Teak also Caulk Pitch covers of Hatch
Ways.
  To put Dead lights in spaces now Vacant two Round ditto extra.
  To Put all Necessary Bulwarks
  To Step and Fit all spars
  To scrape off & Clean down Vessel outside & Inside.
  Paint same & Tar Where required With two coats & Render same in a
satisfactory manner.
  Also New Gammon Iron
  To supply Sixteen Blocks of the Various sizes with pt. Sheaves & Iron
strops where required for the sum of Ninety two Pounds ten shillings.
  Rebolting Rudder.

Dated 17th Day of August 1905.

Extra

Two pieces Frame Timber
Pair of legs & Plates & Bolts – £1.13.0
New Rudder & Ironwork
New Main Boom
Blocks          one of 6" Iron strops
                two jib Sheet Blocks
                six of 5" Double
                two Single
                one – 8" Treble
                eight of 7" Iron strop
                four – 5" single
                one of 6" Block Patent Sheave one of 5" ditto
Block for contract
                8 of 7" Iron Bound Blocks

73

one of 8" "     "       "    Treble
one of 6" "     "       "
one of 9" "     "       "    Double Main Sheet
two of 5" Rope Strop Double
two of 5" "   "    Jib Sheet
one of 5" "   "    Single

## Pilot Boat

(page) 67

| | | £. | s. | d. |
|---|---|---|---|---|
| extra | Four of 5" Double Pt. Sheave at 6/9d. | 1 | 7 | 0 |
| | Five of 5" Single | | 16 | 10½ |
| | Pt. Sheave for 6" Block 2/- | | | |
| | Dead ditto for 5" 9d. | | | |
| | Bulls eye & strop | | 2 | 6 |

(1905)                  (page not costed)

| | |
|---|---|
| Aug 19 | Day to two Men & Theo Shoreing up |
| 21 | Day to Man 1/2 Day to ditto |
| 22 | Day to 2 Men & Prentice 1/2 Day to Self |
| 23 | Day to two Men |
| 24,25,26 | Days to two men |
| 28 | Day to two men |
| 29,30 | Tide to self, three men & 3 Prentices |
| Sept. | |
| 31, 1,2 | Tide to self, three men & 3 Prentices |
| 4 | Day to two men, 1/2 Day to self |
| 5 | Day to man, 1/2 Day ditto & Prentice |
| 6 | Day to three men & 3 Prentices |
| 7, 8 | Day to two men & 3 Prentices |
| 9 1/2 | Day to Self, Prentice & 1/2 Day to Man making leg |
| 11, 12 | Day to two Men & 3 Prentices |
| 13 | Day to Man making Companion Doors |
| 14 | Day to Man & Prentice |
| 15, 16 | Day to two Men & Theo & Prentice |
| | & Day to Jimmy Caulking Deck |
| 18, 19 | Day to Four Men & Four Prentices |
| 20 | Day to Three Men, 1/2 Day to Man |
| | & Day to three Prentices |
| | Day to Man Rudder |
| 21 | Day to Five Men |
| 22 | Day to Four Men & 3 Prentices |
| 23 | Day to three Men, 1/2 Day to Self & 2 Prentices |
| 25 | Day to Man & Day to two Prentices |
| 26 | Day to Man, 1/2 Day to 4 Men & 3 Prentices |
| 27 | 11/2 Day to two Men & 2 Prentices |

| | | | |
|---|---|---|---|
| 28 | Tide to three Men & two Prentices | | |
| 29 | Day to Man, Pilot Boat | | |
| 30 | Day to Man, 1/2 Day to Theo | | |
| Octr. 2,3 4 | Day to Man & 2 Prentices | | |
| 5,6 | Day to two Men & 2 Prentices, Painting Name &c. | | |

(page 69)                                                                £. s. d

1905                                    Pilot Boat/brought For Ironwork

| | | £ | s | d |
|---|---|---:|---:|---:|
| Sept 1st. | New Stem Iron Band & Bolts | | 8 | 0 |
| | Gammon Iron | | 10 | 0 |
| | Tiller &c. | | 4 | 0 |
| | Bulls eye strop | | | 8 |
| | New swivel strop Main sheet | | 4 | 2 |
| | Strop to jib sheet Blcok | | 2 | 0 |
| | Items | | 3 | 6 |
| | Plumbers a/c. | | | |
| | For repairing pump & other Items | | 7 | 3 |
| | | 1 | 19 | 7 |

| | | £ | s | d |
|---|---|---:|---:|---:|
| | extra | | | |
| Sept 21st | Rudder Band spill Plate & Nails | | 1 | 6 |
| | Two leg Bolts Plates & spanner | | 8 | 0 |
| | Labours about Winch Handles &c | | 6 | 0 |
| | 3/4" screw shackle thimbles & Pins for Rigging | | 2 | 3 |
| | Middle strap of Rudder Bolts &c | | 2 | 0 |
| 28th | Spider Band 23/4 Bolts & Nuts | | 1 | 6 |
| | New Topmast Fid | | 1 | 0 |
| | To Plumbers a/c. For 61/2 lbs Brass | | 10 | 7 |
| | Gal Sheet Iron | | | |
| | Labour to same & Locks | | 6 | 9 |
| | | 1 | 19 | 7 |

| | | £ | s | d |
|---|---|---:|---:|---:|
| | To 4 Pairs of Gal Clip Hooks @ 7d | | 3 | 0 |
| | Harbour Dues & Water supplied | | 13 | 10 |
| | To Repairing Pilot Boat Flora | | | |
| | afterward S.A.J. of Newport as per | | | |
| | specification | 92 | 10 | 0 |
| Extra to contract | | | | |
| | New Pair of Legs | 1 | 14 | 6 |
| | New Main Boom New Cleat &c. | 2 | 7 | 6 |
| | New Rudder | 4 | 10 | 0 |

Blocks

| | | | | |
|---|---|---:|---:|---:|
| | Four of 5" Double Pt. Blocks | 1 | 7 | 0 |
| | Five of 5" Single ditto | | 16 | 10½ |
| | Patent Sheave for 6" & Dead ditto 5" | | 2 | 9 |
| | Bulls eye & strop | | 2 | 6 |
| | Four Pairs Gal Clip Hooks | | 3 | 0 |
| Blacksmith Work | | | | |
| | Iron Work for Rudder | | 3 | 6 |
| | Two leg Bolts, Plate & Spanner | | 8 | 0 |
| | Winch Repairing Handles &c (deducted Handles) | | 6 | 0 |
| | Shackles thimbles Pins spider band Band 2 3/4 Bolt & Nutt Topmast Fid &c | | 4 | 0 |
| | Blacksmith Work deducted | | 5 | 0 |
| Plumber's Work | | | | |
| | 7 lbs Brass Plate @ 1/4 | | 9 | 4 |
| | Gal Iron ash Pan | | 2 | 0 |
| | Labour to same | | 6 | 0 |
| | Lead for Mast & Labour | | 3 | 0 |
| | Deducted 2/0 off lead | 105 | 11 | 2½ |

| | | | | | | |
|---|---|---|---|---|---:|---:|
| | Pilots Bill everything included | | | 105 | 11 | 2½ |
| Oct 7th | | | Cash on a/c | 37 | 0 | 0 |
| | | | | 68 | 11 | 2½ |
| Nov 18th | | | Cash on a/c | 50 | 0 | 0 |
| | | | | 18 | 11 | 2½ |
| August 15th 1906 | Cash on a/c | 5  0  0 | | | | |
| Aug 15th 1906 | Balance of a/c up to this date | | | 13 | 11 | 2½ |

CHAPTER FIVE

# Life in a Bristol Channel Pilot Skiff

Historically important though the political and technical aspects of the Bristol Channel Pilotage Service must be, in the final analysis it was the men who put to sea in all winds and weathers to follow a hazardous calling, as pilots, westernmen or apprentices, who made the service what it was and gained for it its enviable reputation. It is fitting therefore to allow some of these men to tell their own story in their own way, since only a first-hand account can give one a genuine 'feel' of the times.

The first is the story of Capt. George Buck, a retired Bristol pilot who served his apprenticeship in the Bristol pilot skiffs during the days of fierce competition prior to the amalgamation of Bristol pilots in 1918. Reading between the lines of his matter-of-fact statements, one comes to realise why these men earned themselves an unrivalled reputation as magnificent seamen, the like of which we may never see again.

Here, then, are some of Capt Buck's recollections of life in the Bristol pilot skiffs in the early part of the century, unaltered save for the occasional introduction of punctuation marks for easier reading.

The average length of the Bristol pilot skiffs in 1908 was about 40 to 50 ft overall, beam 10 to 14 ft, draft 7 to 10 ft, and they used to cruise from Pill to Liverpool, south coast of Ireland, 50 miles SW of the Land's End to Start Point in the English Channel.

I have sailed from Pill on a Wednesday morning for Liverpool, put our pilot on board a steamer bound for Avonmouth, stayed a night in the Canning Dock and arrived back at Pill the following Tuesday morning, a distance of 600 miles. Piloting was full of ups and downs, sometimes earning good money when our luck was in and when our luck was out – nothing. But the average pay when I was on full pay was better than a trademan's ashore and we had our food found, also when we were at home we could get 'hobbles', ie steering ships up or down the river, mooring or unmooring them on arrival or sailing. In those days a hobble was 3s 9d and sometimes you might have to attend on the ship two or three tides to get that 3s 9d because if the ship did not sail you received nothing.

Piloting was also a very risky job as we usually boarded with the punt. The usual method was to ask the captain to put the ship in the position you wanted, across the sea making a lee, then the skiff would sail under her lee, out punt and the pilot and man would row to the ladder. The man in the skiff would get back into the wind again then come back under the lee to pick up the punt in the smooth water. This was not a difficult job in the daytime but at night it required a lot of skill and judgement, as with an empty ship and a fresh wind she would drift to leeward, and if the skiff lost the wind she would drift down on to her.

Before the pilots amalgamated in 1918 it was a cut-throat affair and we would do anything to get to windward of another skiff, but we were all the best of pals ashore. I have known four skiffs leave Pill on a morning tide and race as far as 50 miles SW of the Land's End. At night they would show no lights and by daylight one at a time would be missing, until only one was left and then she had the first chance. But this did not always turn out for the best, as often the one which gave up first had the first ship, since the western skiff would not bother to speak to ships at night, in order to make sure she was the western boat at daybreak.

Another trick in addition to sailing without lights to get to the westward of another skiff was, in a calm, to get out a long sweep and push all night, and it was surprising how she would slip through the water when the sea was smooth with the aid of a big oar. No 17 once chased us up the English Channel as far as Start Point and at daybreak was not in sight. We spoke to a steamer bound for Bristol and he told us he did not want a pilot there. We told him we would come for any pilotage he cared to pay but all we could get from him was 'I don't want a pilot here'. My mate told him we had come purposely for him and he replied 'I did not ask you to come' and was soon out of hailing distance. We started to work back towards the Lizard and the next day we boarded a larger steamer off the Longships. We were away three weeks that trip for one ship and when we arrived home we heard that the steamer which would not stop for us off Start point had picked up his pilot off Lundy Island, but this only happened occasionally.

Once we were hove to about 5 miles SW of the Wolf Rock, the wind had died away to a flat calm, the sea like a mirror, very dark without a cloud in the sky and the stars shining in the water the same as in the sky, all the lighthouses showing their lights all around the horizon and the Lizard light flashing in the sky. I was on 12 to 4 watch when a ship's masthead light came in sight. I took a bearing and saw she would pass a long way to the north of us and, having no wind, the only thing I could do was show the Bristol signal on the flashlight, though as the flashlight was usually used by fishing boats in this area ships generally gave it a wide berth. We were expecting one of Pyman's ships along, called the *Cober*, she being five days out from Gibraltar. I decided to call one of the pilots (we had two on board) and when he came on deck I suggested calling the other pilot, launching the punt and pulling as far as possible to get as close as we could, then to show the flashlight and hail her with the megaphone. We pulled until she was abreast of us, still more than a mile away, showed the flashlight and started to hail her, but eventually had to give up and had started to pull back to the skiff when we saw her port light come in sight and she came towards us, and sure enough it was the *Cober* bound for Bristol. I put the pilot on board and he towed me back to the skiff. The captain told the pilot he was lying in his bunk and heard us hailing 'We are the Bristol pilot', but they had not heard us on the bridge.

The next night we were still in about the same place and still a flat calm. In the 12 to 4 watch I heard my mate come below and tell the other pilot a ship was in sight a long way north. I turned out and suggested another pull, the pilot agreed and this time he took an oar and we made the punt fly through the water, stopping now and again to show the flashlight. We were just deciding to give up when she went hard-a-starboard and steamed towards us. She was bound for Bristol and of course I expected to be towed back to the skiff as we had pulled much farther than the night before, but when the pilot suggested this to the captain he told him had lost a blade and a half of his propeller and wanted to make sure of his tide. The pilot looked over the bridge and told me but I did not care, being happy to think we had another ship, and started to row back. After pulling for some time I stopped to see if I could pick up the skiff's light but with so many stars in the water I could not find it but could see the Wolf light and knew if I pulled in that direction I was bound to find her, also my mate would show a light. It seemed I had been rowing for hours alone in the world and I started singing to keep myself company. Then I stopped rowing, looked around and saw a light and was close to the skiff. My mate was pleased to see me back. The two pilots were E.W. Born and R.M. Stenner, Pilot Born on the *Cober* and Pilot Stenner on the *Clara*, one of Burdock & Cook's ships. When Pilot Stenner rejoined us he said the captain told him he had loaded grain in a Russian Black Sea port and damaged his propeller in the ice and was ten days from Gib when we boarded him. I have often wondered how many miles I pulled that night and thought it strange that it should have happened on two successive nights.

Three weeks after we had boarded these two ships we were cruising off the Longships when an outward-bound steamer hoisted a pilot jack, steamed towards us and asked if we would land three stowaways. We told them to put a ladder over and the pilot would come on board. This we did and he agreed to land them for three pounds and stores enough to last them two or three days. The captain was very generous and in addition to the £3 gave us salt beef, salt pork, hard and soft bread, tobacco and cigarettes. The pilots then decided we would take them to Newlyn and land them, though by doing so we could lose a ship. About four hours after we had taken them on board we arrived at Newlyn and the Customs were there to receive them, having been told by the Coastguard that we had them on board. We stayed the night at Newlyn, left at daylight and put one of our pilots on board a ship for Bristol. The next day another steamer came to us and asked if we would land a stowaway and the pilot agreed to land him for £3. We were off Pendeen Point and the pilot was trying to decide what to do with the stowaway when I saw one of our skiffs coming round the Longships bound up-Channel. I suggested our pilot offer them £1 to land him at Barry and they agreed on condition we said nothing about it.

The skiff was the *Freda*, No 8, and the two men were Sid Thayer and Jim Thomas. The next time we met I asked them what they did with the stowaway and they told me they landed him at Barry as his home was there. It seems he had gone on board to see some pals off, had a few drinks, fell asleep and woke up when the ship was west of Lundy Island. This was the only time I had the experience of taking in stowaways during my ten years in the skiffs and strangely enough both within a couple of days.

I was very happy in the skiffs. It was a fine job in the summer and my father was very keen on fishing, so when it was calm we would fish the bottom anywhere in the Channel with handlines and would catch skate, conger, gurnard, dogfish, mackerel, bream and various other fish. One trip we had my nephew Bert (Pilot Stenner's son) on board for his summer school holidays. We had been to Liverpool and on the way home we were off Anglesey with just enough wind to give us steerage way. At daybreak I put a mackerel line in the water and before it was halfway out I had a mackerel. I went below and whispered to my nephew to come on deck (he was eight years of age) and he was up like a flash when he heard that the mackerel were about. I put out another line and we were pulling them in as fast as we could get the lines out, and in half an hour we had a bucketful and got tired of hauling them in. They were very small, about 8 or 9in long. I told him to carry on with the two lines while I cleaned and boiled some for breakfast, and when I asked him how many he thought he could eat he said 'three'! I boiled eighteen for breakfast and we ate six each. My mate was a much older man than I and he suggested we have another eighteen for dinner, and we enjoyed them also. The weather was very hot with very little wind, so I cleaned another eighteen, split them up the back, put a little pepper and salt on them and laid them on the spars in the sun all day and they were like kippers. At 5pm I started to fry them. I asked Bert how many he wanted and he said three as he did not think he could eat another six. Anyway, I cooked the eighteen and we all went below at 6pm for our meal as it was a calm and no traffic about, and after Bert had eaten three he said he thought he could eat the other three. I pulled his leg many times later when we were both pilots about the time when he ate eighteen mackerel in a day.

We called at many ports around the coast for news, water and stores, etc. On the south side of the Channel it was Ilfracombe (quite a few girls from this little harbour married pilot-boat men, my mother being one of them), Appledore, Padstow, Newquay, St Ives, around the Land's End to Newlyn and Falmouth. On the other side of the Channel it was Barry, Swansea, Tenby, Milford Haven, Fishguard, Holyhead and Liverpool.

There were, of course, many anxious moments during my time in the skiffs, some of them still vivid in my memory, such as the following:

Boarding the ss *Ashby* in the Bristol Channel on a dirty night I went in the punt with the pilot, put him on the ladder and got back to the skiff safely. Getting the punt back on board, we had lifted her forefoot out of the water when the skiff gave a heavy lurch and my mate slipped on the deck, letting go the painter. I could not hold her and she slipped back into the water, filled and was gone in the darkness. We decided to heave-to until daylight, hoping to find her again. We hove dead-to on the starboard tack for half an hour, then half an hour on the port tack, keeping this up until daybreak. We knew she would be to leeward of us, but being full of water and with a heavy sea running we would have to be close to her to see her. Putting the skiff before the wind, we ran half an hour and were thinking we had lost her when, just as we had given up hope of finding her, there she was quite close. We picked up her painter, hove dead-to, got the jib purchase on her stem and hove her up until the water ran out, then lifted her on board, very thankful we had found her, although we had lost the oars and bottom boards. A pilot skiff without her punt was virtually crippled.

Hove to off the Foreland Point in the Bristol Channel, with a strong westerly wind and heavy snow blunts, four rolls in the mainsail, reefed foresail and storm jib and rough sea. A ship's light came in sight and on our showing the Bristol signal with the flashlight, we were answered by the *New York City*, bound for Bristol. We spoke to her and asked her captain to put her head north, which would give us a good lee. This he did and we out punt and I rowed the pilot to the ladder, the sea quite smooth under her lee. The skiff got back into the wind again and was coming back under the ship's lee to pick me up, so when I saw her coming I called to the pilot to go ahead on the engines. I heard the ship's telegraph ring and started to row to leeward but when I looked to see how close the skiff was I could see nothing as a snowstorm had shut out everything. I could only hope I was in a position where the skiff would pass close to me and the only thing I could do was keep the punt head to sea. I was beginning to think I was in for a bad time when I saw a dim glimmer of light and immediately threw the painter which was, as usual, coiled on the thwart. It struck my father in the face and he instantly took a turn around a bitt. As I hopped on board, his first words were: 'I thought I had lost you'. I was like a snowman and he said he had not seen me until the painter hit him in the face.

Our pilot was taking a steamer from Bristol to sea and gave us orders to have the skiff in the river at Pill to take a rope from the ship in order to tow to Barry Roads, a distance of 25 miles. When approaching the roads the wind was increasing and he decided to come on board. We then cast off and as the wind and sea were increasing he decided we would have a quiet night at Barry. It was very dark as we were approaching Barry entrance when suddenly a blue light (a signal for a pilot), was shown from a large ship at anchor in the roads. We sailed off to her and she was the *Everton Grange* (twin-screw) bound for Avonmouth. We hailed her, told them to put a ladder over and we would put a pilot on board.

The weather had by now got worse with a strong west wind and confused sea, with the tide ebbing west. The ship was lying across the tide, with the tide running on her lee side at about three knots. This meant we had to keep well to leeward, drop the punt with the pilot and myself, and the man in the skiff would have to get back into the wind, then come back and pick me up. If he lost the wind under her lee the tide would set the skiff down on the ship and, with her rolling across the tide, do some damage. Everything went along fine. I put the pilot on the ladder and the skiff was coming back to pick me up with sufficient way to take her in to the wind again, and I was about to jump aboard with the painter when the pilot hailed us to come back and take the Liverpool pilot in as he wished to catch the first train back to Liverpool in the morning. I rowed back to the ladder and then saw that the skiff had lost the wind and was setting down on the ship and we could do nothing to stop her going alongside. We managed to get a couple of fenders over and she brought up on the ship's starboard quarter close to the propeller, the tide pinning her there. I made the punt fast to the skiff and asked them to pass us down a rope to heave us clear of the ship's quarter as every time she rolled she smashed our bulwarks and the propeller was very close. But before we got the rope the propeller started to revolve and we yelled for them to stop it. The engines were stopped right away, they passed us down a rope and as they hove us amidships the pilot looked over the ship's side and asked what all the shouting was about. I told him we were close to the propeller and felt sure it had touched our bottom. The pilot, using the ship's engines, then brought her head to tide and we were able to sail away from her.

I pulled up the floorboards in the steerage to make sure we were not making water as the blades of the propeller had been whizzing round abreast our cockpit. When we found everything was all right we asked if the Liverpool pilot still wanted us to land him. The reply being 'Yes', I rowed back to the ladder and took him in, but as soon as I started to row towards the skiff he said he would rather go back to the ladder. The skiff was getting close, so I told him it was best to go to her as I did not want that experience again. We got alongside and hauled the punt on board, set more sail and as we shaped course for Avonmouth I made a pot of tea.

When we settled down, the Liverpool pilot started to give me a lecture which went something like this: 'George my son, chuck it, I would not go back in that punt again under those conditions if they gave me the ship, and if I had a son who wanted to go into that service I would rather shoot him.' This went on until we reached Avonmouth when we put the punt out and I landed him on the old pier in the river. He shook my hand, thanked me, gave me a golden sovereign, and as he turned to walk up the steps, he again said, 'George my son, chuck it before it is too late.' I never saw him again, but served another eight years in the old skiffs.

The next day the pilot came on board to survey the damage. It was not serious, about six feet of bulwark damaged. We pulled up the floor-boards over the pump-well and found she had not made any water. The pilot then asked me why I had been shouting and I told him if he had been on board the skiff with that propeller churning round alongside he also would have done some shouting and I was still of the opinion that the propeller had touched our bottom. About three weeks later we put her on Ilfracombe Strand to scrub and tar her bottom and we found the bottom scored like a piece of pork for three feet to a depth of half an inch on the two strakes above the garboard strake. The pilot was my brother-in-law, R.M. Stenner, and the westernman, my father. During the ten years I was in the skiffs it was the only time I was really frightened. The ship had been part cargo and the blades of the propeller partly out of the water.

Once we were cruising about thirty miles west of Lundy Island in strong westerly wind and rough sea, expecting the Dominion liner, *Manxman*. We knew there were no skiffs to the westward of us and if she came along she would be ours. We had three rolls in the mainsail, reefed foresail and storm jib. About midday the pilot decided to run towards the island as the wind was increasing, as sometimes, when blowing hard, the wind would decrease to leeward, but when we got abreast the north end of Lundy the wind increased, so, putting another roll in the mainsail, we decided to run farther up Channel. About 8 pm we rolled the mainsail down with the jaws of the gaff on the mainboom, double reefed the foresail and hove-to, being now between the Nash and Foreland Point.

We never cared to give up the chance of a ship and we were certain if she (the *Manxman*) came along she would be ours and, being a large ship and loaded, we should manage to board her. At 10 pm the pilot came on deck and the wind seemed to be increasing, with heavy squalls and confused sea, so he told me to put the helm up and run for Barry Roads. This skiff was the old *Glance* and she would run in any sea and never take any water over the stern. Just before midnight the pilot came on deck again, told me to make a pot of tea and call my mate. This I did and was on my way to the cockpit with a cup for the pilot when I heard a crash, and when I got to the cockpit I found that the mainboom had snapped like a carrot. The mainsheet and the end of the boom were towing in the water and the mainsail was in ribbons. We had a difficult job getting the broken piece of boom on board and were afraid it might hit the side and break a plank, but we finally got everything secured and again running before the wind. I thought we should go to Barry but the pilot said we would go to Pill as we would require a new mainsail and mainboom.

Lowering the foresail and jib, we put a spare foresail fore side of the mast, hoisted it up and were away like a scalded cat. When we reached the river we hoisted the reaching foresail aft side of the mast for a mainsail, set the foresail and arrived at Pill just before high water, and while we were mooring the havenmaster's office hailed the boatman's shelter to say that the *Manxman* was in King Road and had asked for a pilot. We had not only lost a mainsail and mainboom but also a good paying ship. This was just the luck of the draw in the days of competitive piloting.

During the 1914–18 war we were racing for a hospital ship just below Barry Roads against No 8, *Freda*. The ship was about three miles away and we had a lead of about a quarter of a mile and if anything were a little faster then the *Freda*. The wind was fresh with a nasty head sea and we were carrying whole mainsail, foresail and middle jib. When they saw they could not catch us, they set their topsail, so we immediately set ours and were still faster – the ship was ours for certain until, almost in hail of her, we hit a nasty head sea and our masthead went over the side and the topsail, gaff and all the gear attached to it was towing in the water. The mast broke just below the hounds of the rigging and we were afraid the masthead or gaff might put a hole in our side, so No 8 passed us and put their pilot on board the ship and we could see the nurses and wounded lining the rails, having a grandstand view of the contest.

After No 8 had put their pilot on board they came back to us and asked if they could assist us, but by this time we had all the gear aboard and secured. However, although we had about 20ft of mast, we had no gear on it with which to hoist a sail, so we asked her to tow us into smooth water, where I decided I could climb the mast, drive a large spike down into it and then secure two small blocks to the spike to enable us to set a couple of sails. They towed us to Cardiff Roads where the water was smooth and offered to tow us to Pill, but our pilot thanked them and said we would manage as we knew they had another pilot on board and wanted to go to the westward.

We got two pieces of pointline, put a small eye in each, lashed a hammer, spike and two small blocks with lines rove through around my waist, then put the two pieces of pointline around the mast. Then, by pushing one piece at a time, I was able to get to the top of the mast and drive the spike into it, make fast the blocks so that we were able to set the foresail and a small sail abaft the mast for a mainsail. We then waited for the flood tide, hove up the anchor and arrived at Pill at high water.

One day in March 1918 we left Barry at 7pm with a moderate east wind and sea with good visibility and ebb tide. We hove-to just west of Breaksea LV and decided we would have the daylight chance between the Nash Point and Foreland Point. The pilot (A. Chiswell) and myself went below at 8pm and were discussing the ships due when we heard my mate call out 'Look out where you are going!' The pilot went on deck and I followed him not thinking there was any danger, but when we got in the cockpit we saw a steamer quite close coming stem on into us; we could do nothing and she struck us amidships on the port side. I looked below and could see the sea rushing through the side and knew it would be only minutes before she sank. No one spoke; the pilot and my mate went forward and I stood on the stern, knowing that as soon as she hit us it was every man for himself. I thought when she sank that I would be able to dive into the water and perhaps hang on to the edge of one of the steamer's plates until someone passed down a line. Although it could have only been a matter of seconds as this went through my mind I did not feel scared.

Looking up at the ship's stem, I saw a movement although it was very dark, so I called to my mate and he answered and said he was sitting on the ship's starboard anchor. I ran along the deck and could just reach the anchor, pulled myself up, at the same time calling to the pilot, asking where he was. He replied that he was on the port anchor and the *Greta* slowly sank down under the steamer's stem. It could have been only two or three minutes from the time of the collision until she sank.

We could not reach the deck from the anchor. Then we saw a face looking down at us and I asked for a line and was passed down a fender lanyard and we were quickly on deck but we could hear the pilot calling for help. I spoke to him and he said he wanted a ladder as he was hanging on with his arms, and to hurry as he could not hang on much longer. I sent the sailor for a ladder and meanwhile passed the eye of a small mooring wire down to him telling him to try and get his foot into it and take the weight off his arms. He was able to do this and when the ladder came along he was soon on deck. He went to the bridge and the captain told him he would land us at Mount's Bay (Cornwall) but our pilot insisted that he put us on board an examination vessel which was in the vicinity, which he did and they landed us at Barry the next morning, where we caught a train home.

A few days afterwards Pilot Stenner came and asked me if I would get the *Mary*, No 17, ready for sea. He had asked her owner, Pilot Carey, for permission to work her as she was laid up for want of crew. She was a fine skiff about the same size as the *Greta* and he told me he had asked an uncle of mine to be my mate. We went to Pilot Carey's house for the sails and running gear and in a few more days we had her ready for sea and were away again with Pilot Chiswell as second pilot. The sinking of the *Greta* was almost forgotten, though Pilot Chiswell said he would never forget hanging on to that anchor by his arms; he was over sixty years of age and weighed 15 stone!

These were about the most anxious times I had during the ten years I was with Pilot Stenner, but when boarding ships at night during dirty weather, we were always glad when we had the punt back on board. In the daytime we took little notice of the weather and it had to be very bad when we could not board and it was not very often we had to run for shelter. The skiffs were fine craft and in bad weather would heave-to with the fore sheet to windward and the helm lashed a little down and would work to windward off a lee shore. I was with Pilot Stenner from 1908 to 1918 and also spent my school summer holidays with him when he was westernman in my Uncle William Hunt's skiff, No 13.

During the year 1910 I started to learn the Morse and semaphore, the only lamp we had being an old bicycle lamp lighted with colza oil, and used my cap up and down to make the dots and dashes. It had a fine clear glass and I could get an answer from a ship a couple of miles away, but at this time the Morse code was not much in use and usually it was only the large ships which answered us. It was a great help, as otherwise we had to sail close to every ship and hail her, asking where bound. It was not an easy job holding the lamp in one hand, using the cap with the other and steering with your back to the tiller, especially if it was rough and the skiff jumping about. When Morse got more common, it saved a great deal of time and work, as we would call a ship and if answered, would send, 'Where bound?' If the answer was unfavourable, we would just reply,'Thanks' and this saved quite a lot of wear and tear on sails and gear. I even got our pilot interested in Morse and he soon was able to send 'where bound?' If the reply was Bristol or Avonmouth, he could manage to read it but that was about all he could manage.

We were about four miles off Start Point in the English Channel one night when I heard my mate come below and whisper to the pilot that a ship was calling us in Morse. It was very calm and quiet and I heard them light the bicycle lamp. A few minutes later I heard him say 'I don't know what he is doing', then I heard him spell out a few letters but it was nothing like Bristol or Avonmouth and I was dozing off to sleep again when he started off with 'M-A-N-I' and again said 'I don't know what he is doing'. Athough I was half asleep it suddenly came to me that I had seen one of Brocklebank's ships in the Bristol paper at Hull called the *Manipur*. I jumped out of my bunk, ran on deck, took the bicycle lamp and morsed '*Manipur*, we are the Avonmouth pilot.' She immediately went hard-a-port and steamed to us, otherwise she would have passed us at least two miles away. We should not have had that ship but for the old bicycle lamp and she was a good paying ship to us. When we arrived home the pilot gave me an electric torch and I was able to improve my signalling. We then had many ships which would have passed us but for the use of Morse.

I also got very efficient with the semaphore and sometimes would run up the letter 'J' on the signal halyards when off the south end of Lundy Island and ask Lloyds to wire home for news of ships. When they had a reply they would hoist the letter 'J' and we would sail close in, run up the answering pennant and take the message. This often saved us the time of going to port for news.

On one occasion we were cruising off the Land's End, having been away a week with lots of fog and not knowing what ships had passed up. We did not want to go into port for news, which might mean missing a ship, but fresh bread was getting short. The pilot decided to sail inside the Longships, send the punt ashore, send a wire home and wait for a reply. I moored the punt alongside the quay at the little harbour at Sennen Cove, went to the post office and sent my wire. I knew I should have at least an hour to wait, so thought I would stroll up to the naval signal station to while away the time. The signalman on watch made me welcome, gave me a cup of tea and I explained to him what I was doing. We could see the skiff hove-to about half a mile offshore. He asked me if I could semaphore and when I told him I could he suggested that if I did not want to hang around I could go to the post office, ask them to phone the message to the signal station and he would semaphore the message to the skiff. I thanked him, went to the post office, made arrangements for them to phone the message to the signal station, bought four loaves of bread, filled a breaker with fresh water, rowed back to the skiff and explained what I had done. We pulled the punt on board and were able to keep a watch for any ships which might come our way.

About two hours afterwards we saw the letter 'J' hoisted at the signal station and we received the message. It was quite a long one and one ship's name I could not get, so I asked the pilot to let me go ashore again to make sure. I walked up to the signal station again and obtained the name of the ship. I was in no hurry and was yarning with the signalman when a naval officer came in and asked what I was doing there. I told him I had made a mistake with the name of one of the ships in the message; I could see at once I should not have told him. He gave both me and the signalman a good telling-off and said he did not want the signal station to be responsible for wrong messages. I forget all he said but he made me feel very small, so I told him I was very sorry and it was of no importance; we only wanted to know what ships were due. He got very interested and we had a long chat and he finished up by telling me that any time we wanted a message sent they would oblige us. The ship was the tanker *Pattella*, four days from Gib bound for Avonmouth, and that night we put the pilot on board, whereas if we had gone to harbour for news we should have missed her. The choice of harbours would have been Newlyn or St. Ives.

After some years 'deep sea', I eventually obtained my pilot's licence in 1927 and retired in 1953, but I shall never forget those days – and nights – in the old sailing skiffs.

Capt. Buck is a typical product of a traditional piloting family of Pill and the following family tree serves to illustrate the continuity of the profession, which in some cases has persisted right into the present day.

## A Pill Family of Seafarers

James Cox, born 17 August 1798, Bristol Channel Pilot 1831.
Wife Sarah, born 4 February 1807.

---

### Children
Ann, born 3 February 1826, married John Smith, Bristol Channel Pilot. Sons: Thomas, Master Mariner; Sydney, Bristol Channel Channel; Frank, 1st Mate's Cert. Grandson; Sydney Smith, Master Mariner.

---

Rachel, born 20 May 1828, married James Buck, Bristol Channel Pilot. Daughter: Ellen, married William Hunt, Bristol Channel Pilot (widower) with son, William Hunt, Bristol Channel Pilot, two grand-sons, Edgar, Bristol Channel Pilot; Cyril, Bristol Channel Pilot and Master Mariner. Granddaughter: Mabel Buck,married Robert Stenner, Bristol Channel Pilot. Grandson: George Buck, Bristol Channel Pilot, Master Mariner and Hon Life Member of the Company of Master Mariners of Australia, married Emily Born, daughter of Edmund Born, Bristol Channel Pilot and Master Mariner.

Great Grandsons: Robert Stenner, Bristol Channel Pilot and Master Mariner; Wlifred and Dennis Buck, Bristol Channel Pilots with 1st Mate's Certs; Edgar Buck, pilot's apprentice lost at sea whilst serving as 3rd officer in tanker *Cadillac*, torpedoed 1 March 1941, aged 25. Stanley Buck, pilot's apprentice invalided out after three years' service.

Grandson: James Cox Buck, enlisted in Kitchener's Army August 1914, killed in action on the Somme, 16 September 1916, Sgt. 7th Batt. Som. L.I. aged 25.

---

Ellen, born 21 April 1830, married Joseph Hunt, Boatman. Sons: Fred and Thomas, Master Mariners. Grandson: Thomas, Bristol Channel Pilot and Master Mariner. _____

Eliza, born 3 December 1831, spinster. _____

Augusta, born 18 November 1833, married Samuel Callaway, Boatman, no children. _____
Sarah, born 30 September 1835, married James Hazell, Boatman. No sons.

---

James, born 5 December 1838. Son: James Cox, Master Mariner. Daughter: Edith, married Samuel Buck, Bristol Channel Pilot. Grandson: Maurice Buck, Bristol Channel Pilot and Master Mariner. Edith Cox was Rachel's niece, and Samuel Buck was James Buck's nephew.

In 1953 James Cox had six grandsons in the Bristol Pilot Service, great grandsons, George Buck, Maurice Buck and Thomas Hunt, great-great grandsons Wilfred Buck, Robert Stenner and Denis Buck.

Today (September 1969) only one, Denis Buck remains in the service and no more apprentices to carry on the family tradition.

There has survived an interesting log-cum-account book, kept by Pilot James Cox in the years 1831 to 1838. To quote Graham Farr:

> Between the lines of its methodical entries one can visualize the duties of a pilot of his day, though not the hardships.[1] Cox was born in 1798, received his branch certificate in 1831 and is believed to have been drowned in 1839 when his skiff (the *Echo*, built by Hilhouse at Bristol in 1835) was lost in the Bristol Channel. A typical entry from his book is as follows:

11th October 1838, the French brig *Julia*, 84 tons

| | |
|---|---|
| To my Pilotage from the Bason to Kingroad | 0 10 0 |
| To 1 Yaul and 4 men from do. to do. | 0 18 0 |
| To 2 Horses and 1 Driver | 0 11 0 |
| To my Pilotage from Kingroad to Lundy | 2 10 0 |
| To Haven Master's Fee | 0  1 0 |
| | £4 10 0 |

From this it will be seen that, apart from pilotage, the pilot was responsible for towing arrangements in the river. Bristol was late in adopting systematic steam towing and, incidentally, when the tug *Fury* was introduced in 1836 there were riots, led by Pill men, and the offending vessel was boarded with force and cut adrift. In the earlier years of Cox's piloting career the horse and towing yaul method was at its height. Most vessels were handled by one yaul and three or four men, but there were cases of up to three yauls and fourteen men, doubtless depending on the size of the towed vessel and the state of the tide. The standard fee for the usual tow, from King Road to the 'Bason', was 3s 9d for each man and 3s for the yaul, plus an allowance of beer. Where towing horses were used, usually two and one driver, the standard fee was 5s per horse and 1s for the driver.

The pilot cannot be said to have reaped a fat living. The fee for taking the largest ships from King Road to Lundy was £6 6s, but large ships were few when shared among the thirty-four or so pilots of the port, and, taking large and small, he never reached an average of one ship per week. His largest single fee was probably for a job of salvage, for he received £35 for taking the French brig *Hermione* into Ilfracombe. Once he took a yacht to Weymouth for a fee of £16, and another time he piloted a brig of 373 tons from Lundy to Liverpool for £5 5s. On many occasions he was pleased to accept 10s as an assistant pilot and occasionally a 'dotage' of 5s. Occasionally he was quarantined for nine or ten days on board a ship he had piloted in, and for this he received 7s 6d a day. In 1835, 1836 and 1838 he spent about six weeks of the year fishing for mackerel, a practice which the authorities encouraged, probably because Bristol did not have a considerable fishing population.[2] Cox's earnings for each of the complete years 1832 to 1838 are tabulated below. They exclude fees for towage, etc, which he handled but had to disburse later.

|  | Own Income | | | Pilotage | |
|  | From Pilotage | From Fishing | | | Half fee and misc |
| Year | £ s. d. | £ s. d. | Tonnage | No of jobs | jobs |
|---|---|---|---|---|---|
| 1832 | 80 12 9 | ——— | 5026 | 41 | 3 |
| 1833 | 85 6 6 | ——— | 4910 | 34 | 4 |
| 1834 | 105 11 6 | ——— | 4715 | 23 | 5 |
| 1835 | 78 12 0 | 31 10 0 | 4496 | 17 | 2 |
| 1836 | 162 14 6 | 27 13 0 | 7586 | 29 | 4 |
| 1837 | 122 15 6 | ——— | 5088 | 26 | 7 |
| 1838 | 186 8 11 | 23 12 6 | 6917 | 30 | 8 |

Although there was bitter rivalry between the Bristol pilots and those of the Welsh ports there was also surprisingly strong ties, for we find that as the Welsh ports gained importance, many representatives of old established Bristol pilot families moved across the Bristol Channel to take Welsh licences.

For instance the families of Ray, Gilmore, Adams and Comerford became Newport pilots, the Hooks, Crosses, Scarretts, Smiths, Thomases and Bucks went to Penarth and the Humphreys, Paynes and Cases to Cardiff. Also, there was a great deal of intermarrying between the pilot families of Bristol and Wales. Thus, because until recent years the profession followed a strong father to son tradition, the same surnames were perpetuated in the pilot lists on both sides of the water for many years.

It is interesting note that a Rowles (of the Pill family of boat builders) was serving as a Welsh pilot in the 1970s. Likewise there are to be found representatives of the same Welsh pilot families in all the pilot ports from Gloucester to Port Talbot, as well as Bristol.

NOTES

1.  I am indebted to Mr. Maurice P. Buck for the loan of this book and for permission to use these extracts.
2.  Bounties were offered in the famine years of 1795 and 1801 to all and sundry who could bring fish to Bristol for sale in the open market. Pilots were offered additional bounties by the Society of Merchant Venturers.

# CHAPTER SIX

# A Newport Pilot Remembers

The second account, reprinted by permission from a 1961 issue of *Sea Breezes*, is that of Capt W. Bartlett, who served his apprenticeship in his brother's cutter *Foam* and then went deep-sea, first in sail and then in steam.

Obtaining his square-rigged master's certificate, he sailed as master before returning to the pilotage service and retired as general manager of the Newport pilots in 1956:

I began my apprenticeship in the Newport-Monmouth pilotage sevice on 23 January 1906 at the age of fourteen years and two months, bound apprentice to my older brother, Simon, who was twenty years my senior and had been a pilot then for three or four years. The cutter which he owned was named the *Foam*, formerly the *Polly*, built by Mordey Carney of Newport. She was a fine sea boat but years of battering around in the Bristol Channel and a severe stranding had weakened her fastenings, and she leaked like a basket. She had the added disadvantage of being one of the slowest boats in Newport.

At this time there were forty-four pilots in the port, some of whom had permission from the Pilotage Board (as it was then called) to sail with another pilot, and there were about thirty-six pilot cutters, each owned by an individual pilot. A typical cutter was about 50ft overall, with a beam of 14ft 6in and a draft of 8ft to 9ft. All ballast was inside. As the name implies, these boats were cutter-rigged, with a mast about 50ft from deck to truck; main boom 30ft long; gaff about 23ft long, and bowsprit 20ft to 25ft long.

Roller reefing was nearly always fitted to the mainsail, the hoist of which was about 25ft. The staysail had two reef bands and the sliding bowsprit was run in or out according to the size of jib carried. With this rig, the one hand on deck could reduce sail from whole mainsail, staysail and first jib, down to six rolls on the mainsail, double reefed staysail and storm jib, without any help from the pilot or watch below. Indeed he was expected to do so, and the same applied when making sail. Although these were the normal working sails, the cutter carried in addition a balloon staysail, gaff topsail and a spinnaker, which would be set when required. The cutters varied considerably in their capabilities; some would be at their best in bad weather, some in fine, some close-hauled, some running free. It depended chiefly on where they were built.

Mordey Carney of Newport turned out good sea boats which could give an account of themselves in heavy weather, but they had no turn of speed. In my opinion, the best all round boats were those built in Porthleven, in Cornwall. Two of these were the *Spray* and the *Hope*, which were later of Barry and then of Bristol. As an apprentice, I thought these two were the best boats in Newport. James Angear of Looe also built some of the cutters, of which I remember the *Maud*, and the *Idler* (later renamed *Dawn*) which was built for my brother.

From Fleetwood came the *Alpha* which was very fast but would not stand up to being pressed in heavy weather. Perhaps the most out-standing boat in Newport was the composite-built *Mascotte*. Owned, designed, and to a large extent built, by Pilot Thomas Cox and his son, also Thomas, she was larger than any other cutter, being some 56ft overall. I believe she had railway irons for frames and also 'screw rigging', which was unheard of up to then in the pilot cutters. She looked a very capable boat although I never saw her pressed very hard, but I think this was due to the temperament of the pilot rather than to any fault of the boat.

The running gear followed a uniform pattern in all the cutters, the head sheets, mainsheets, main and peak halyards leading along to the cockpit. This was so that the sheets could be worked without leaving the cockpit, or the halyards could be let-go in case of an emergency. The tackles for setting them up were in relatively the same position in all the boats.

The cockpits were from 5 to 6ft long, 4 or 5ft wide at the fore end, tapering to 2 to 3 ft at the after end, with a depth of 2ft 6in below deck level and coamings 18in high above the deck. They were self-draining. A companion led from the cockpit to the cabin, with a high step between the cockpit and the companion ladder. There was a small hatch forward of the mast, immediately above the sail locker. Skylights were not favoured as they were considered to weaken the structure of the boat. Strong towing bitts were provided forward, together with a windlass or capstan for the anchor. On the port side of the deck the dinghy (always known as the punt) was stowed. About 10ft long, 4ft 6in beam, with a narrow keel, square stern and a very full midship section, the punt was very light and a splendid sea boat.

Below deck the cutters were divided into forecastle and cabin. In the forecastle were a coal-burning cooking range, water tank, chain locker, coal locker, sail locker, bunk(s) and storage for food and crockery. In the cabin were the pilot's bunk, settees, cupboards and a slow-combustion stove for winter use. Between the cabin and the companion ladder to the cockpit were the 'runs' where the mooring ropes and fenders were stowed.

In order to qualify for a pilot's licence one first had to serve a five-year apprenticeship in the cutters. During this time wages ranged from 5s a week in the first year to £1 a week in the last year, the pilot providing the apprentice with food and bedding while afloat. When his apprentice-ship was finished the intending pilot had to serve twelve months in a foreign-going square-rigged sailing ship, followed by twelve months in a foreign-going steamship. After this it was merely a question of await-ing one's turn for a vacancy to occur; the position on the waiting list was governed by the date of signing indentures.

At that time this period of waiting varied from ten to fifteen years. Some ex-apprentices preferred to remain at sea, obtained their certifi-cates and served as officers or masters of ships. Some went as dock pilots, skippers of tugs, or into other jobs connected with shipping. Yet others went back immediately into the pilot boats as boatmen, or 'pilots' men', as the local directory described them. In addition to these ex-apprentices there were a number of men who had served the whole of their working life in the pilot cutters. Together the pilot's men and the apprentices manned the cutters, the manning of each individual cutter depending on the way the pilot chose to work.

When at last the ex-apprentice had completed his waiting time till a vacancy occured he was examined by the examination committee of the pilotage board with regard to his qualifications. This committee reported their findings to the full board, and, if these were satisfactory, a licence would be granted to pilot any class of ship between Lundy Island and King Road, and to or from the port of Newport. The newly licensed pilot usually bought a second-hand boat as soon as he could afford it. Then he was his own master to go out when he liked and come home when he liked. He could go north, south, east or west, with no one to bother him except the other pilots, or perhaps his wife if he did not bring in sufficient money.

The pilots could be divided into categories depending on the way they worked. First, there were the 'cinchers' – I don't know how this name was derived – who worked around the river mouth or went to Bristol for ships from that area. They worked quite hard in their own way and were among the best pilots for handling the deeply-loaded ships that went to the various wharves in the river. Any ships that they had from the west were usually those that other pilots did not want. They manned their boats with one apprentice, in which case they would sail the cutter to Bristol Pilots' Pill and there await a ship coming to Newport from Bristol or Avonmouth. Alternatively, they rowed the punt out to the river's mouth at Newport and when they picked up a ship, towed the punt back up the river. On the occasions when they did have two apprentices, or an apprentice and a man, they would work in much the same way, only then the pilot himself did not have to row.

Second, there were the 'crack-of-dawn boys' who worked from Barry. They spent the hours of darkness in Barry Harbour and went out at daybreak for a chance of ships that had come past the pilots to the westward in the dark without having seen them. They also looked for ships which had come to Barry Roads for orders and were now bound for Newport. When the barometer was falling they would see that they had good moorings out and spend their time tapping them and predicting what terrible weather the pilots who were outside were going to have. They worked hard (or at least their crews did) in a humbugging sort of way, furling and setting sail and beating around in Barry Roads, watching other pilots go to the westward of them and board ships. I suppose it suited their temperament and they made a living out of it. Their crew would be a man and an apprentice.

The next group, forming the bulk of the pilots, covers a much wider range. They would go out at any time and some of them would stop out in quite bad weather, but each individual pilot had certain limits both as regards weather and distance beyond which he did not care to go. During the day one of them might go beyond his distance to keep below another pilot, but after dark he would give up and return to his favourite hunting ground. They might refuse a medium-size ship when there was a big one due, or they might take a small one just ahead of a big one. After a while it was possible to predict how each one would act under a given set of conditions. Once again their crew would be a man and an apprentice.

Finally, there were the 'western-going men', who tried to specialise in the bigger and better class of ships. If there were two or three of them looking for the same ship, they might end up in Liverpool or Belfast or off Dungeness. I have heard of Bristol pilots being a couple of hundred miles out to the WNW of Brow Head looking for the *Royal Edward* or the *Royal George*. I myself have been up off Dungeness, several times to Liverpool, and as far as the North Channel. These boats usually carried two men. If they had one man and an apprentice, it was only when the apprentice had enough experience to be reliable, otherwise they would have to carry two men and an apprentice.

This was a specialised job and the men who manned these cutters were specialists at that job. Each man had to sail his cutter as if she were racing in a regatta in fine weather or foul, year in year out, and get the utmost out of her. He had to keep in the track of shipping, seeing that he was in the right position for hailing a ship without losing any more ground than was absolutely necessary. He had to manoeuvre to the right position for casting the punt adrift and picking her up again after the pilot had boarded the ship. All this was in addition to the ordinary hazards of the sea. The navigation of the cutters would have made a deep-water man's hair stand on end. No logs were ever streamed and no log-books were ever kept, but it was seldom that the boats were put ashore. If that did happen it was through standing in too near the shore in light winds to dodge the tide.

I cannot speak too highly of the pilots' men. They could do any sailorising job that came along, and could turn out a hot meal under almost any conditions. For most of my apprenticeship we had a man called Billy Beckett who was always referred to by the other men as 'Billy Iron Head' because he never wore a hat of any description. He was the finest shipmate I ever had; he trusted me, taught me, encouraged me and shielded me in every way. He might not have washed as often as some people would have liked, but, bless his salt-encrusted old face, I added this to his virtues, as every drop of water we used I had to carry on my shoulder in a cask from the quay down a flight of slippery steps to the cutter. Thus to me it was a valuable commodity not to be wasted on washing faces. Years afterwards, when I first came to Newport as master of a ship, he came down to see me and I was able to thank him for all he had done for me. In his turn he was pleased to tell me how right he had always been about me.

My brother, although he had such a slow and leaky boat, was one of the western-going pilots and a pretty tough one at that. 'Bad weather is our chance – that's when ships want pilots most' was one of his favourite sayings, and of the faster boats he would say, 'Well, if we can't go as fast we can go as far.' Standing 5ft 2½in. tall nothing ever daunted him and he would work all the hours there were.

When I began my apprenticeship he had two men and myself in the cutter, but he hated to think of the boat lying idle while the men had a couple of days' rest, so less than twelve months after this he decided that the boat could be worked with one of the crew ashore resting and the other two afloat. In this way neither he nor the boat would be idle at all. The idea was that we should 'work short', as he called it, that is to say about down to Lundy Island and he would take any ship of which he had a chance.

On one cruise my brother, with Billy Beckett and myself as crew, was below Lundy, and there was no one below us; we were the 'westernmost boat' as we called it. Unfortunately the weather was bad – strong south-west wind visiblity poor with rain and mist, and sea rough. In fact it was so rough that my brother told Billy Beckett that it was too bad for me to go with him in the punt to board a ship and not to bother to speak to anything which came along. Now Billy Beckett did not believe in dog watches; the watch was from 6pm till midnight – very nice when it was your watch below but an awful long time on deck.

As it was my watch on deck this night, there I went, more to keep a lookout than anything else. I had not been there long when I sighted a steamer coming up which I thought would pass close to us, so I called my brother. Both he and Billy Beckett, who had not yet turned in, came up on deck and summed up the position. As we were going to be so close they decided to speak to her. She was a big ship in ballast bound to Newport, the *Sandon Hall*, straight from the builders on the north-east coast. Beckett wanted to 'stop' her but my brother still thought it was too rough.

Billy said: 'Don't be a fool. He's got his head screwed on all right and he's a good kid in the punt. After all, what are we doing down here if it's not to board ships?' My brother was persuaded and went below to change, while I put my life-waistcoat on (a very special and infrequently used precaution this) and made the punt ready. Before we set off my brother gave me his pocket whistle, not as a parting gift, but to blow if I should manage to get myself back into a position to be picked up by the cutter again. Off we went into the black night with myself sculling over the stern with the 9ft 6in single oar, the way the punt was always propelled.

I got the punt up to the pilot ladder on the *Sandon Hall*, my brother scrambled up, and I sculled back to the cutter where my mate Billy picked me up at the first attempt. The punt was hoisted in, more sail set, the mainsheet eased off and away we went. I took the helm and Billy told me to keep her straight before the wind. If I let her gybe he told me I should have the mast out of her, and if I let her swing the other way she would go on the rocks and we should both be 'chewing gravel' by the morning, which was his delicate way of saying we should be drowned. I asked him where we were, and he replied 'between Trevose and Lundy', which gave him a range of about twenty miles. I followed this by asking how far off shore we were, to which he replied 'A tidy distance'.

Having thus reassured me on the dangers besetting us and pinpointed our position, he went below, telling me to call him if I was in doubt about anything. If I had carried out his last instruction, I should have called him before he got to the ladder, but I had to prove I was a man and take some responsibility (it was October 1906 and I had had my fifteenth birthday two days before), but it did lay heavy upon my shoulders. One moment the cutter would be on the point of gybing, the next she would be heading towards the land, and I could see the crests of the seas out ahead breaking on a lee shore. It seemed to go on for hours and hours, when at last I saw a steamer's lights inside our track, and the south end of Lundy showed up on the port bow. With this, all my troubles vanished, as it was no longer necessary to run dead before the wind and, taking a turn with the tiller rope I went below to call Billy Beckett. To my surprise I found that I had only been on deck for just over an hour. I told Billy that everything was all right and that I had sighted Lundy on the port bow. He came up on deck and took the helm while I made myself a cup of cocoa and had a couple of cabin biscuits with plenty of butter and strawberry jam. This, together with dreams of how Billy would tell my brother and all the other pilots' men and apprentices what a good lad I was, passed the remainder of the watch pleasantly.

We had our own Rule of the Road, which was to give way to everything. Masters and officers of ships seemed to know about it and it usually worked all right. Sometimes in a calm a ship might cause us some anxious moments, but we were a small target and were usually missed somehow or other. Pilot cutters on the wind would not make one gybe to keep clear. Fog horns were not sounded to an approaching steamer, the generally accepted theory being that if you did, he would not know what class of sailing craft you were and might take violent evasive action. In this case you might not get near enough to hail him. The usual thing in fog was to approach the steamer on a broad bearing to the course which you expected him to be steering. The steamer's whistle signals would be kept right ahead until the cutter was close enough for the steamer to hear the pilot's call.

In order to make a good living a pilot had to work hard and know what he was doing. There was no point in slogging down the Channel to get westernmost boat, and boarding a small steamer just ahead of one that would pay three or four times as much in dues. It was necessary to know which ships were due, and when. A pilot could then work out how long he would have to wait before a big ship came along and what his chances were of having her.

Information regarding the movements of ships bound to Newport was supplied to the pilots by two shipping butchers' runners. The charge was a shilling a list, a red-hot tip being worth more. New ships on the list were specially marked, as in this case a pilot who had left the previous day would not know about them. Elliot's list was considered to be reliable, with plenty of inside information, but Ford's was reputed to have just been copied from one of the shipping newspapers. Armed with these two lists, the *Liverpool Journal of Commerce* and the *Cardiff Journal of Commerce*, a pilot could decide on his course of action. He would take into consideration which ports the ships were coming from, whether they would be on the north or south side of the Channel, which pilots were already out, and whether they would know about these ships. From all this information the pilot would decide which side of the Channel and where he wished to go and instruct his crew accordingly. Even so, luck played a very important part in piloting.

I can recall a trip I had with my brother before I began my apprenticeship. We went to Liverpool, which pleased me greatly as I had always wanted to see the big liners. When we arrived, however, we found that there was already another pilot there for the ship that was bound to Newport. A telegram home produced the reply that the *City of Karachi* (which was a new ship) was leaving Belfast shortly, and another steamer called the *Admiral Nelson* was leaving Dublin the following week. We set off in a gale for Belfast, but later the wind died out and we had only got as far as the North Channel when the *City of Karachi* was due on her way to Newport.

It was dark when we saw the lights of two steamers simultaneously. We could have gone to either one, but there was not time to go to both. Unfortunately we chose the wrong one, so that was another ship lost to us. After this we went to Dublin for the *Admiral Nelson*. She was still in port there but had just had her orders changed from Newport to Glasgow. Next we went across to Holyhead where we heard that the

*Tugela* was leaving Glasgow for Newport. Now we were not allowed to make an appointment with a ship at any particular place, but we used to get round this by sending a reply-paid telegram to ask when the ship was leaving. When the reply was received we would work out when the ship would be along and wait in her probable track. This we did with the *Tugela* and picked her up in a very dense fog. The tow round to Newport was in very dirty weather. When we arrived I was able to start school again the following day, having been three weeks away. The pilotage inwards was £13 15s – a very meagre return for three weeks work.

Piloting could, however, be a profitable business if the pilot was prepared to work hard enough to make it so. During the five years that I was serving my apprenticeship my brother had the following income:

| | |
|---|---|
| 1906 | £584 |
| 1907 | £687 |
| 1908 | £771 |
| 1909 | £559 (six weeks lost in taking delivery of a new cutter) |
| 1910 | £663 |

With these figures (an average of £653 a year) we were in the top six, and one or two years were nearly at the head of the list. This was at a time when the master of a foreign-going ship drew £15 per month in wages. Pilotage was settled twice a month and Simon's best account was in March 1908, when he earned £60 6s 6d, made up as follows:

| | | |
|---|---|---|
| February 29 | *Monza* out from Newport to the Nash | £7 0s 0d |
| March 1 | *Royston Grange* off Caldy inwards | £12 0s 0d |
| March 7 | *Yangtze* off St Govan lightvessel inwards | £14 10s 0d |
| March 12 | *Mark Lane* | £ 3 10 |
| March 14 | Royston Grange outward | £12 0s 0d |
| March 14 | *Yangtze* outwards | £14 10s 0d |
| | | £63 10 |
| Various deductions (pilotage board, etc) | | £3 3s 6d |
| | Earnings | £60 6s 6d |

Of course these earnings did not go straight into the pilot's pocket. It cost between £300 and £350 per year to run the cutter. My brother's weekly expenses were made up as follows:-

| | |
|---|---|
| Wages (apprentice and man) | £2 10s 0d |
| Provisions | £2  0s 0d |
| Rope and sails | 10s 0d |
| Insurance | 10s 0d |
| Incidentals | 10s 0d |
| | £6  0s 0d |

Also at the back of the pilot's mind was the thought that he might have to buy a new cutter one day. When my brother bought the *Idler* in 1909 she cost him £245.

Whenever I told anybody of the pilotage service when I was serving my time, it has often given rise to the comment that it was a dangerous job for a lad to go out in a 10-ft punt on a dark night and then have to find his way back to the cutter without having anyone to tell him what to do. I suppose it was dangerous, but in those days it never struck me as being so. My one hope on turning in was that I should be called to board a large ship. After all, to board a ship was the climax of the whole operation; to fail in that meant that all the previous efforts were wasted.

On 6 March 1908 we were anchored at Milford and it was blowing a strong gale, according to my brother's diary. I can remember that the storm staysail was bent, the topmast housed, and the trysail was got up on deck. However, my brother decided that it would be difficult to beat out under a trysail as there was such a sea in the entrance. Accordingly, at midnight, we sailed under six rolls in the mainsail, storm staysail, and storm jib, and boarded the *Yangtsze* at 5am off St Govan lightvessel. There was no question of remaining in harbour and letting this ship go, the only question was how best to get out of Milford to board her.

The following illustrates how little my brother thought of heavy weather. On 31 August/1 September 1908 heavy gales were reported around the British Isles and according to the local newspaper winds of 70 mph were experienced at Newport (I think this was the night the sailing ship *Amazon* was lost near Port Talbot and the *Vera Jean* went ashore near Barry). The entries in my brother's diary read as follows:

| | | |
|---|---|---|
| August 30 | 1908 | Off Boscastle. |
| August 31 | 1908 | Up off Hartland. Strong westerly wind. |
| September 1 | 1908 | Ran up. Lost mainsail and boom. Went into Barry. |
| September 2 | 1908 | Raining hard, getting mainboom made. |
| September 3 | 1908 | Overhauling damage done in breeze. |

One of my worst nightmares is to be sailing a cutter up the side of a sea as high as a five-storey building without being able to get enough way on to reach the crest.

When meeting and boarding a vessel the procedure would be as follows. The watch on deck would hail the ship when the cutter was close enough to find out if she was bound for Newport. If so, and she was one that the pilot would take, the watch would tell the ship to stop. Meanwhile the pilot and the watch below would turn out, the pilot dressed in his shore-going clothes and the man would take the helm while the apprentice was getting the punt ready. The cutter would be sailed up under the ship's lee, but not too close, or the wind would be lost and the ship blow down on the cutter. That required the most careful judgment, taking into consideration wind, sail being carried, speed, and leeway being made by the ship. To get too close created a far more dangerous position than being too far off.

After the apprentice had taken the gripes off the punt and made the painter fast on the fore side of the rigging, he would lift the fore end out of the chocks and the helmsman, taking a turn with the tiller-rope, would get out of the cockpit and lift the stern of the punt on to the rail (which was about 18in above the deck). Then, listing the punt inboard, she would be slid over into the sea. It was of course preferable to do this on the lee side, but if this was not possible the cutter would be run dead before the sea at the moment of launching. The pilot and apprentice scrambled aboard and the man would veer her astern of the cutter until in the best position for letting-go. After this the pilot would pull in the painter, putting the end handy for the apprentice, who was meanwhile sculling for the ship's ladder, using the single 9ft 6in oar over the stern.

Arriving alongside the ship, the pilot would watch his chance, and when the ship finished her roll towards him would grab the ladder and climb up. The apprentice would then scull away from the ship as hard as possible. Meanwhile the man would be manoeuvring the cutter into position for picking up the punt, endeavouring to heave-to in the same position as before. The apprentice would scull towards the hove-to cutter, cross her bows, and, when in the trough of a sea, swing the punt around head to sea and work alongside about amidships. He would then get on board, taking the painter with him, and hoist the punt on deck. No lights were ever carried in the punt as they had been tried and failed, and usually only one oar because a spare one took up so much room. Life waistcoats were looked upon as a sign of nerves. The chief thing was to keep a cool head and not get flustered.

When a pilot docked a ship she was his to take out again, conse-quently his movements were somewhat restricted by having to be at home when the ship was ready for sailing. If a ship was sailing in a couple of days the pilot concerned would go seeking for that time and take anything he had a chance of, and it was possible to work for two months or so in this manner without looking for any ship in particular or going very far. This applied to all the western-going men and it was sometimes a pleasant surprise to find one of them coming up with a small ship, leaving you first chance of a big ship which was due in a day or so. Some of the pilots had a working agreement to look out for each other's ships if they were home. This did not work very well however as it was never certain if they would be home, and of course you could not expect them to stay ashore and look out for your ship for nothing.

The pilots' men acquired a wonderful memory for the appearance of other pilot cutters and of steamers, memorising the silhouettes of many ships and also their outstanding features. Pilot boats could be identified by the cut of their sails. This all helped for identification at long range, which was most important.

On one occasion we were off Pendeen about the middle of December. All the ships on our list had gone up Channel, except one called the *Corby*. She was our last hope until we went into port and obtained another list of vessels bound to Newport. In the middle watch, two steamers showed up, one with a single masthead light, near the shore, and one with two masthead lights, well off. The outside one was the best chance and I started to stand off to her, when I suddenly remembered that I had seen the *Corby* somewhere before and she only had short pole masts and would not carry a mainmasthead light. I went about and just managed to get to the inside ship with the single mast light and the *Corby* she proved to be.

If when two steamers came along together (and that seemed to happen very often) you chose the wrong one, it was not the last that you heard about it. When the pilots met ashore they would tell each other which ships they had had, where they had boarded them and when. Then when your pilot returned to the cutter he would want an explanation as to how you had managed to miss a ship which was boarded twenty miles further in from where you had been. It was looked upon as a terrible tragedy if you missed a ship which you had been looking for, even if you had one that paid only a few pounds less afterwards.

I have mentioned that there was no restriction on the movements of the pilots, but this is not quite true, as once a year there was an inspection of the cutters by the Pilotage Board. This was known as 'Show Day', although it actually lasted for two days. On the first day all the pilot cutters, with the exception of four which were allowed off in rotation each year to keep the ships moving in and out of the port, were assembled at Newport Pilots' Pill. Here an inspection of all the gear and equipment was made by members of the Board. On the following day the cutters would be under sail in the river and the Pilotage Board would review them, steaming past in one of P. & A. Campbell's passenger steamers hired for the occasion. Each cutter would be gleaming with new paint, the mast and spars scraped, the brasswork highly polished, and the gear aloft in spanking condition.

The inspection usually followed the annual overhaul, which in our case as well as in a number of others, took place at the yard of P.K. Harris, Appledore. I must hasten to add that the fact that the *Foam* leaked so badly was no reflection on their workmanship, which was of the very best, but was owing to the fastenings being weak, and for some reason or other this was never put in hand. I once remarked to Billy Beckett that she never took any heavy water on deck and he explained that this was because it all went through her sides before it could reach the deck! Still the life was an interesting, exciting and hard one, with some danger thrown in. The apprentice was part of the crew and had to take his share of responsibility, which made him feel a man.

I finished serving my apprenticeship in 1911 and went away 'deep-sea'. By the time I returned to the pilotage with my master's certificate, the individual independent pilots and their sailing cutters were gone for ever. They were swept away by the First World War and replaced by the pilotage service of today. My brother Simon died in 1918, after having his whole way of life changed. He fought hard against the amalgamation of the pilots and some years ago when I was looking through his papers I found a sheet of paper on which he had begun to set down arguments against the new pilotage service. He had only written the words 'I shall lose my freedom' – there was nothing else on the sheet. Those five words contained the germ of the old Bristol Channel pilots' outlook on life.

# CHAPTER SEVEN

# Sixty Years of Barry Pilotage

Lewis Alexander of Barry was one of the last Welsh pilots to have a cutter built for himself, the *Kindly Light* in 1911. His background is worth relating, for it is typical of so many men who followed the sea until the First World War brought irrevocable changes to all sea-going communities around the British Isles.

One of a family of nine, he reached the age of eleven in 1878 (the permitted school leaving age of those days) and, like most boys of his time, had to start contributing to the family income. It came as no surprise, therefore, when his father, a Cardiff hobbling pilot, announced one day that he had 'got a ship for Lewis' – the little sail/steam three-masted auxiliary schooner *Bessie* – and young Lewis was to be her cabin-boy.

A day or two later, the *Bessie* had completed loading and was ready to sail, so her newest and youngest crew member arrived at the West Dock, Cardiff, complete with his sea-bag and 'donkey's breakfast': a very excited small boy setting foot for the first time on board a vessel as a paid hand and on the threshold of a career which was to last for over sixty years.

His father stayed with the *Bessie* until she was below Penarth Head and then dropped into his own boat. As he fell astern, one can imagine the mixed feelings of both father and son, the one anxious yet resigned, the other torn at leaving home yet proud of his first job at sea. The *Bessie*'s engineer probably added to the small boy's trepidation by shouting, quite untruthfully and to Lewis's utter disgust, 'He's crying already after you!' Nevertheless, he confessed many years later that, as they passed Lundy, he lay in his bunk and gazed at the rough timbers of the deck-head, thinking longingly of his mother and home.

From Barry the *Bessie* went to Garston where Lewis's attention was drawn to the enormous hulk of Brunel's *Great Eastern*, which was in process of being broken up.

Another poignant insight into a youngster's first reactions to being away from home is gained from Lewis Alexander's own description '. . . we had our orders for Barrow-in-Furness, where I received a letter from my mother, chastising me very severely for not having written before. I had made an attempt at Britton Ferry, but it was midsummer and I felt the heat – the paper became limp and dirty with the sweat of my hands, together with the nib of the pen, which would catch the paper and

Pilot yawls in Barry harbour, early 1900s. [courtesy N Alexander]

splash the ink over the letter, so I gave it up. In my mother's letter I had a very severe scolding and this phrase remains in my mind to this day, "What did I send you to school for?"'

After about three months of coasting the eleven-year-old Lewis had his first taste of danger when the *Bessie*, on passage from Cork to the Bristol Channel, found the tide setting her onto the rocks of the Smalls. Like many small auxiliary vessels of her type, she had neither the engine power nor adequate sail plan to get her out of trouble. The helm was put over and all hands held their breath until, fortunately, she eventually cleared the rocks – just.

A member of a real seafaring family, Lewis had two uncles, both Cardiff port pilots (known sometimes as 'thumpers'), whose job it was to board ships coming into Penarth or Cardiff Roads without a Channel pilot on board. From their anchorage under the 'Kymin' (Penarth Pier) they worked only within the Roads, not having qualified as first-class Channel pilots. Mainly they took the smaller craft which, in the heyday of Welsh coal, steel and ore, numbered hundreds and provided them with a reasonable living. Between them they employed about a dozen men as assistants and in due time, Lewis Alexander joined a port pilot as cabin-boy at the weekly wage of two shillings and sixpence. Thus he began to build up experience towards his ultimate career.

This was the zenith of the Welsh sailing pilot era and Lewis Alexander's recollections of the boats and the men are interesting. Recalling that there were well over a hundred qualified first-class Channel pilots at that time and between eighty and ninety boats of various descriptions, he remembers big, powerful boats like the *Papelio* and John Morgan's *Cardiffian* down to 'little flat-sterned' boats similar possibly to his own first boat, the *White Heather*, which was a converted Cornish fishing lugger. Some of the most well known and best of the fleet were the *Papelio*, the *Amelia*, the *Excell*, the *Polly*, the *Grace Darling* and the *Minnie L.* At that time the *Polly* was generally regarded as the fastest boat, which probably accounted for her pilot, Thomas Williams, being nicknamed 'Slippery'.

If the *Polly* was queen of the fleet, then Thomas Williams was the doyen of the pilots – with his broad-brimmed, low-crowned 'Holy Joe' hat, so typical of a pilot's headgear in those days. Lewis Alexander recollects '. . . it was very picturesque to behold a boat coming along on the wind with the pilot in one of these hats worn a little shabby, with the lee flap beating to the wind just like the foot of a mains'l.

In remembering the dominant characters among the pilots, he pays particular tribute to John Morgan and his fine Hambly-built cutter *Cardiffian*. As a professional seaman who must himself have faced danger a thousand times, it was high tribute indeed that Lewis Alexander could still say 'When I think of John Morgan, that courageous man . . .', and then go on to recall examples both of his bravery and of his apparently psychic powers.

109

Lewis Alexander's first boat, the *White Heather*, originally a Cornish fishing lugger. [courtesy N Alexander]

One wild winter evening, down off the North Cornish coast the *Cardiffian* was being hammered by a rising westerly gale and John Morgan decided to go into Padstow Harbour for the night to rest his men and himself. Padstow has a very difficult entrance and is (to quote Alexander's understatement) 'Not easy to take in a westerly gale', but the *Cardiffian* made it safely and was soon made fast alongside the wall. Sails were stowed, a meal prepared and all was snug for the night. It so happened, however, that there was a loaf of bread on a locker close to John Morgan's bunk, and he had not been long turned in when it inexplicably fell to the deck. Morgan got up and replaced it on the locker, rather surprised since the vessel was lying quietly and there seemed to be no reason for its falling. Back in his bunk again, and the loaf again fell to the deck. Once again he replaced it but when the same thing happened twice more he finally recognised it as a sign and, rousing his men, he said 'Get ready for sea. We must sail immediately.' 'But Boss, it's blowing harder now than when we came in,' they said. 'Never mind,' he replied, 'Something tells me we must be at sea tonight,' and so the cutter beat her way out of the shelter of Padstow into the teeth of the now furious gale. All night they sailed according to Morgan's instinct and in the first faint light of dawn they sighted something resembling a dismasted vessel lying under Hartland. It proved to be a barge, one of a pair being towed out to the Brazils which had broken adrift from her tow. As the *Cardiffian* drew near, Morgan and his crew could make out human figures on board the barge, helplessly drifting down to the rocks of that granite-bound coast. At great risk to themselves and despite the difficulties caused by the heavy seas they managed to put a line aboard the barge and to tow her off – no mean feat in itself as it was a beat to windward. The tow rope parted after a short while but John Morgan managed to connect up again and, once around Hartland Point, was able to bear away for Ilfracombe where the barge was taken over by an ocean-going tug, the *Pathfinder*, and her crew handed over to the care of the local Missions to Seamen. And when John Morgan applied to the consignees of the barges for the replacement cost of his broken tow rope, they self-righteously protested that they had 'Never heard before of a British seaman seeking payment for saving life at sea!' and refused to reimburse him.

John Morgan's psychic insight was demonstrated again one evening when he had returned to his home mooring, stowed up and gone home with his sons, who were his crew. They had not been in the house long enough to get a meal when Morgan became restless, eventually saying, 'Come on boys, back to the boat. We are going to sea.' His sons protested that there was no food aboard and they had not yet eaten. 'Don't worry,' he replied, 'we shall be back by morning.' So to sea they went and in due course, approaching the Somerset shore, they spotted something in Porlock Bay. It proved to be a Cardiff pilot cutter, the *Elsie J*, dismasted and being swept rapidly inshore by the strong current. 'That's what we came to sea for,' said Morgan and, without hesitation, sailed the *Cardiffian* between the crippled vessel and the rocks, passed his line and towed her safely home.

This was typical of the man who, in his earlier years, in about 1878, had earned the Royal National Lifeboat Institution's medal for saving the crew of a schooner ashore on the Cardiff Sand. The Penarth Lifeboat crew were not available, so John Morgan rounded up a scratch crew among the local pilot boys and fishermen, broke into the lifeboat house and launched her to the rescue. In all, John Morgan saved thirty-nine lives with his own cutter and in one of his last jobs provided yet further evidence of his quality as a seaman, as well as underlining the ever-present dangers of the sea-going life. He was around the Land's End (or, 'Round the Land', as the pilots phrased it) and well up in the English Channel when he boarded a steamer bound for Cardiff. As they headed towards Falmouth the wind rose to a full gale from the south-west until the vessel, unable to head up to it, drove in until it became obvious that she was going ashore. The captain was desperate but John Morgan's lifetime of experience came to their aid when he persuaded him to flood the after-hold. Although he had never heard of such a thing before, the captain did so and with her engine going full speed astern and her head to the cliffs the steamer just managed to hold her own throughout the night until dawn brought an abatement in the weather and she eventually arrived safely in Cardiff.

Alexander stayed with the port pilots for about two years and then his father had him apprenticed to a Channel pilot named Horatio Davis, a 'hard case with a grey whisker'. Horatio Davis was a double-licence pilot – one qualified for both Cardiff and Barry – but Lewis's apprenticeship was to be for Barry, provided that boy and pilot suited each other after a trial period. Accordingly he joined the cutter *Wave* at Ely Harbour and was greeted on board, 'not very enthusiastically', by Davis's assistant, William Gandy – 'a fair complexioned man with a reddish whisker, a hard case he was, too'. As they sailed past Barry on his first trip 'with little or no wind' there was a pilot boat anchored inside of them and, to test the boy, the pilot asked if he could identify her. 'No 45, John Dalling, Sir,' replied Lewis, much to the satisfaction of the pilot, as the highly competitive nature of the job made it essential to be able to identify any rival at long range. He stressed the importance of keeping a constant look-out all around the compass, whereas in the port pilot boat it had only been necessary to look out over Lavernock Point.

So the weeks went by until Horatio Davis eventually agreed to consolidate Lewis's apprenticeship – but even then, only on a three months' trial. This was because a pilot was very dependent upon his crew and it was usually the apprentice who took the boarding punt to and from the ships. Obviously, therefore, the apprentice had to be completely reliable at all times.

Lewis proved satisfactory and became a fully-fledged indentured apprentice pilot on 15 December 1895, being forbidden to enter 'taverns, ale-houses, theatres or music-

The *Kindly Light* tows her punt into the lee of a ship before putting her pilot on board. [courtesy N Alexander]

Pilot Zachariah Wyke's Cardiff pilot yawl No.7, *Lead On*, which was later sunk in a night collision. [courtesy N Alexander]

Pilot Lewis Alexander
(right) on his cutter
*Kindly Light.* [courtesy
N Alexander]

halls'. But, in compensation he was given a thorough grounding for his future profession in the hardest and most exacting of schools, learning among other things to scull and row a tiny punt in all sorts of conditions at sea, and to 'hand, reef and steer' in the pilot cutter. And reefing in the *Wave* meant doing it the old way, fighting the heavy mainsail down cringle by cringle and tying reef points, while the boom crashed and banged from side to side – and as the *Wave*'s boom over hung the counter by about four or five feet, to get down the first cringle involved climbing out on the main sheet. When Lewis joined her, the *Wave* had already lost a man doing this and it is no wonder that most of the pilots eventually adopted the new patent 'Appledore' roller reefing gear, even though it meant restricting the boom length and therefore the size of the mainsail.

Lewis Alexander also gives us an insight into the domestic lives of the pilots of his day. As in any other community, there were the good and the bad, the fortunate and the less fortunate, the conscientious and the lazy. The pilot who owned the cutter *Papelio*, for instance, 'did not get on very well at home' and one day announced to his wife that he 'was going away for three months.' Accordingly he boarded his boat, put to sea and no one ever knew where he went, though he eventually turned up in Milford Haven. Funds were by then running low so it was perhaps fortunate for him that a trawler ran into and damaged the stern of the *Papelio*, which brought him a few pounds in compensation. Then away he went again, down to the Long Ships and Cape Cornwall, not seeking work but just sailing aimlessly.

One morning when his men had cooked breakfast and gone on deck to call him he sighted a steamer close by and just starting to move away, having waited in vain for the pilot to make some move to board her. She went on up-Channel to find another pilot and later reported the incident to the Cardiff port authority. The pilotage authority also came to hear about it and 'were most concerned' at the damage to their reputation and that of the Bristol Channel pilot service in general. They threatened that if the *Papelio* did not return immediately they would send a tug to bring her in. However, the pilot eventually came back of his own accord, the *Papelio* was impounded and a writ nailed to her mast. When she was later put up for sale she was bought by a pilot named Jimmy Duggan and was eventually run down and sunk off the Cornish coast. Duggan himself survived to replace her with a Plymouth cutter called the *Active*, 'a very long vessel' and one which worked until the Cardiff pilot service amalgamated and converted to powered craft.

In talking of the men and their boats, Lewis Alexander reflects that the two always came to mind together, 'the man and his boat' – the one so much a part of the other. One such pair was Abraham Woodward (pronounced Wood'ard) and the *Excell*, which had been built to outsail the famous *Polly* of 'Slippery' Tom Williams. When the *Polly* was run down by the schooner *Mistletoe* in 1892 or 1893 she was abandoned by Williams and his crew, who were taken aboard the schooner. Next morning the

Some of the Cardiff fleet in its heyday around 1900, possibly assembled for Review Day. [courtesy Graham Brooks, whose grandfather, Thomas Herbert Brooks, owned and worked cutter no.13, the EVB shown fifth from right.]

*Polly* was sighted off Ilfracombe and the lifeboat brought her into that harbour from where she was towed back to Cardiff by William Tucker's tug the *Lady Salisbury*.

Because Williams was in financial difficulties, Tucker had the *Polly* repaired and fitted out on the understanding that Williams would work her and pay him back. To use Lewis Alexander's own delightful phraseology, 'this did not come to pass' and so the *Polly* was placed into the hands of the 'bums' (bailiffs) for sale, and bought by Giles Woodward, brother of Abraham who had the *Excell*. Giles worked her until he retired and then handed her over to his son, Giles the younger, who in turn sold her when the Cardiff pilots amalgamated in 1912.

In all the pilot ports, regattas and review days were great occasions and, again to quote Lewis Alexander, 'It was a thrilling sight to behold the vessels dressed for the occasion', and as he recalled the ceremonial sail-past, the boats' names came off his tongue like poetry '. . . *Polly*, *Excell*, *Fanny*, *Grace Darling*, *Marguerite*, *L.J.J.*, *Alarm*, *Iolanthe*' – and those only just a few of the hundred or more which took part. Sometimes, he recalled, the Gloucester boats would enter the review with the pilots, as did Newport vessels such as the *Spray*, *Jubilee* and *Mascotte*, together with others from Barry – *Victoria*, *Hope*, *Bonito* and the *Faith*. The Gloucester boats included the *Berkeley Castle*, the *Alaska* and the *Alert*.

Other gatherings of this size often took place after a period of gales when the weather moderated sufficiently to allow ships to put to sea, and it must have been a memorable sight to see fifty or sixty pilot cutters making sail to race – not for fun but for their very livelihood. So keen then was the race to westward that many a ship in the Roads would be passed by the leaders and left to be boarded by the tail-enders of the fleet, for such was the intense spirit of competition among the pilots that they would continue the contest right around the Land's End and up into the English Channel, so long as there was a chance of finding a ship.

Then came the equally gruelling race home, for the sooner the cutter got home, the sooner she could go seeking again. If the weather was favourable, a homeward-bound ship with a pilot on board would often take his cutter in tow – a practice popular with the pilot but not always with his crew, who had to steer her while the ship proceeded at her normal speed. Under those conditions it needed considerable strength, skill and concentration to steer the cutter, whose foredeck would often be completely submerged under her own abnormal bow-wave.

Towing at night had its additional hazards, as illustrated by yet another reminiscence by Lewis Alexander, who tells of a night down Channel, when the Cardiff pilot, Zacharia Wyke and his assistant, Jasper Matthews, in the fine cutter *Lead On*, spoke an inward-bound ship. She took Wyke as her pilot and gave his cutter a rope in order to tow her up.

During the night, the *Lead On*'s all-round white masthead light went out unnoticed by her crew so that she was invisible to another cutter, the *Gladys*, who also hailed the steamer. Learning that there was already a pilot on board, the *Gladys* bore away to pass under the stern of the ship and hit the *Lead On* just to the foreside of her mast and both vessels sank. Fortunately the two crews, five in all, managed to get aboard one of the cutters' punts – a 13ft pulling dinghy – and pulled all night in a heavy sea and a strong wind. In the morning they were sighted, picked up by a schooner and landed at Swansea after having been given up for lost.

Lewis Alexander claims that the pilot service of the Bristol Channel was (and still is) the finest in the world and recalls many occasions when, on boarding a ship in wild conditions, the captain has said, 'Pilot, I wouldn't have boarded this ship for the value of the vessel'. And indeed many a life was lost in attempting to board a ship from a tiny punt in bad weather.

Though it was usually the boy's job to take the pilot to the ship, when conditions were very bad the pilot would sometimes go on his own, boarding the ship and leaving the punt to be picked up by the cutter. This in itself was a most difficult task for a man and a boy, because a pilot punt was necessarily a heavily built craft and getting her on board the cutter in a heavy sea was no mean feat even after they had captured her.

Occasionally the pilot, having boarded the ship, would persuade the captain to take his punt on board rather than risk losing her. This was resorted to only in the worst conditions of weather, and even then reluctantly because the cutter was compelled to return to her home port instead of waiting down Channel for the pilot to return on an outward-bound vessel.

Lewis Alexander recalls that on one occasion, after he had had to leave his empty punt to be picked up by his man, the pilot cutter arrived home before the steamer he had boarded! Such was the quality of these fine craft.

By the very nature of their calling, a sailing pilot and his crew were shipmates in constant danger. The very operation of transferring a pilot to or from a ship in bad weather was fraught with peril and required a high degree of skill, seamanship and courage. Sometimes over-confidence would result in disaster, as in the case of an apprentice one wild night off Barry. The boy chose to ignore, or failed to take in, the sound advice given him before taking his pilot to a ship in the Roads and, having successfully completed the outward journey, allowed himself to be blown out of the protective lee of the steamer. Powerless before the strong wind and out of sight of the cutter, he eventually stranded on the beach of Sully Island and there died from exposure.

On another occasion, Lewis Alexander recalls that a colleague, Pilot Jack Thomas, was boarding a steamer below the Foreland from his cutter, the *Winnie* (later called the *Bonito*), accompanied by his assistant – a man called Guest. The punt capsized in the heavy sea and although Guest tried to assist the pilot, he could not hold him. Fighting to save his own life, he regained the cutter while Thomas perished.

Some time previously Pilot Thomas had been aboard the steamer *Drum Cruel* off Lundy, bound for Cardiff, when the Newport pilot, Ray, in his cutter, the *Carlotta*, hailed the steamer and asked for a passage up, as he was due to take the ship on to Newport from Cardiff. The ship hove-to and the *Carlotta*, carrying a little too much canvas for the prevailing conditions, did the unusual in launching her punt on the weather side. Although the steamer had little or no way on her, the sea was violently swirling around her bow and the punt capsized in the confused water, throwing out both Ray and his apprentice, Gould. Ray got on to the bottom of the punt and the *Carlotta* sailed alongside to pick him up but failed to do so and he slid off the boat to drown. Meanwhile, the apprentice Gould managed to get alongside the ship where, instead of a ladder, a rope was sent down to him. He got it around his wrists and was hauled up to the rail but his strength then failed and he fell back into the sea. There, he dragged along the ship's side to the counter and the second mate went down in a bowline in an attempt to rescue him, but the frantic boy grabbed him so dangerously that the second mate had to kick him off. Thus both pilot and apprentice were lost.

Sometimes it was an error of judgement which caused disaster, as in the case of Tom Goodman's *Ethel* which was run down by the ship he was about to board, off Ilfracombe. The apprentice aboard was Goodman's son and despite his attempts to save his father they went down together, while the other two men aboard, the second pilot, Jack Morse and Jim Buck, clung to the bottom of the punt until they were picked up.

Although the pilotage regulations demanded that life-jackets be carried aboard all the cutters, the evidence seems to show that they were, in fact, seldom worn. They would, of course, have been the cumbersome, old fashioned cork type and would have made the boat handling difficult. Also it was considered by some that to wear a life-jacket was a sign of weakness, particularly among the boys and younger men, and there is no doubt that this mistaken sense of pride cost a number of lives that would otherwise have been saved.

In 1904 Lewis Alexander, with eight others, took his examination to become a Barry pilot. He was one of four to gain his first-class licence, while five qualified as second-class. For about three years and nine months they worked together as a team – an interesting anticipation of the general amalgamation of 1912 – but they eventually broke up into groups of three, Lewis's partners being Pilots Hancock and Hampson. In due course Hampson broke away and bought his own boat, leaving his erstwhile partners to find another. They eventually found a little Cornish lugger called the *Marjorie* and had her converted to a pilot cutter by her previous owner, a man called Slade, and she served them well for a further three years or so until, in June 1911, Lewis was made up to a full Channel pilot, which made it desirable for him to have a vessel of his own.

He had long admired the *Alpha* of Newport but her owners jealously refused to give him any information as to where she had been built. The *Alpha* was (and at the time of

119

writing, still is) a very fine craft and her owners, naturally enough, were not anxious to introduce competition to themselves. However, Lewis eventually discovered that she had been built at Fleetwood in 1904 by Liver & Wilding, so he decided to go to Fleetwood for his own craft. Meanwhile Mr Stober, the foreman-builder responsible for the *Alpha*, had transferred to another Fleetwood yard, Armour Brothers, and as Lewis wanted the same qualities built into his own vessel it was to this yard that he went for the *Kindly Light*, as she was to be called. In the fashion of the day, all the local seafaring men had an opinion to offer in the building of a new boat and discussion with the Fleetwood pilots resulted in a cutter eighteen inches longer on the waterline and six inches greater in beam than the *Alpha*, at a cost of £500. So, in November 1911, with a brand new boat and high ambitions, Lewis Alexander went to work, but for the first few months he was not as fortunate as he might have been. However, he battled through and later became very successful indeed.

The sailing pilots, before amalgamation, were of necessity hard men and although at daggers drawn at sea, respected each other where respect was warranted and were not without pity for a man fallen on hard times. So it was that Lewis Alexander one day in March 1914 came upon one of his erstwhile partners who, because of drunkeness, had not been able to get a job for many weeks. No one would sail with him and no other pilot would take him to sea, until Lewis took pity on him and agreed to take him seeking a ship.

Like many sailors, Lewis disliked sailing on a Friday (and this was the 13th), but being anxious to help his unfortunate colleague without delay, he put aside his superstition and set off to sea, his crew being the brothers Ernie and Tom Morgan (sons of the famous John Morgan) and a boy. This was in March and as they sailed down Channel the sky was 'very green and forbidding and clouds were working up'. Off the Nash, Lewis decided to heave-to for the night, being the most westward boat and having no immediate prospect of a ship, but when he came on deck next morning he was surprised to find the cutter *White Heather* to the westward of him. So without further ado he set off in pursuit of her, but she boarded a ship before he could catch her, and was left to sail on in search of another.

Off the Foreland he sighted the pilot cutter *Bonito* but she was no match for the *Kindly Light* and soon went 'hard up for home', leaving him the field once again. But shortly afterwards the cutter *Cariad* appeared below him, having adopted the unscrupulous tactic of towing down below a competitor with a steamer. This was greatly frowned upon by the sailing pilots who had their own strict code of fair play. Then the expected gale arrived, with blinding rain which reduced visibility to a matter of yards. When it cleared the *Cariad*, too, had run for home.

Lewis Alexander and his men had not eaten for many hours, so they lay-to on the starboard tack to rest and to eat. There were four new earthenware mugs on the forecastle table – a fairly common occurrence as mugs were frequently broken and the men refused to drink out of enamel ones – and as the hot tea was poured into them, one started to whistle, as some earthenware vessels will do.

Now the Morgan brothers came from a Spiritualist family and to them the whistling mug was such a bad omen that both refused to drink from it. However, the 'guest' pilot said that *he* was not superstitious and took it without demur.

Not long after this, a Barry-bound ship was spoken and stopped to receive the pilot, lying-to so as to give the cutter a lee as she launched her punt. It was Tom Morgan who went with the pilot and they had scarcely cleared the cutter when his brother on board suddenly shouted to Lewis Alexander, who was at the helm, 'My God! Skipper, they're gone and we're going too!' Lewis looked aft and was horrified to see the steamer falling broadside, off a huge combing sea, apparently right on top of them. In fact she did not do so, but the *Kindly Light* broached-to in the deep trough and shipped a great deal of water. Meanwhile the punt had capsized and both occupants immediately turned over on to their backs and floated for some minutes. Then the pilot was seen to turn over, face down, and they knew that he was finished. Tom Morgan had got into a lifebuoy thrown to him from the ship and the *Kindly Light* sailed around to pick him up, still sluggish with the great quantity of water she had shipped. But she managed to get within a line's throw of Morgan and after he had been hauled aboard the body of the pilot was picked up and taken back to Barry.

Notwithstanding such tragic episodes, a pilot's life was not all gloom and as a highly successful man in his profession, Lewis Alexander continued for many happy years to pilot ships in and out of the treacherous Bristol Channel. He saw the final transition of the sailing ship to the steam and motor vessel, and of the sailing cutter to powerful launches, though still referred to as 'cutters'. In his latter days he piloted ships of a type that would have made the skipper of the old auxiliary schooner *Bessie* gasp with disbelief. And, fortunately for posterity, he lived on into an age of technology that made it possible for his son to get his father's life story, in his own words, on tape, and it is upon this that the foregoing account has been based.

Lewis Alexander never lost his early ability to remember the names of the pilots and their boats, as witnessed by Mr R.J.H. Lloyd of the National Museum of Wales who was able to produce, accurately, a list of well over 100 names given him by Lewis without reference to a single note. The list related to the year 1890 and Lewis could even remember details of changes of ownership among the boats, which in itself was remarkable since they changed hands very frequently.

During the same interview he also mentioned the interesting fact that the Channel pilots at one time tried to boycott Barry owing to the poor rates paid. To overcome this, the railway company formed a nucleus of ten or eleven pilots of their own.

The Barry pilots amalgamated in 1915 but this was opposed for a time by a small group, including Lewis Alexander, who continued to work independently. It was not long, however, before their stolid individualism had to give way to the new system

So begins a new era. Three steam cutters at Barry, the Bristol *Queen Mother* on the inside. [courtesy PBA]

and they were obliged to conform with all the other pilots and work to a rota from a steam cutter.

An interesting footnote to this biography of Lewis Alexander is provided by one of his own apprentices, the late Albert H. Austin. Writing in the *Daily Telegraph* of 16 September 1967, in response to a letter about the yacht *Theodora* (ex-pilot cutter *Kindly Light*), Mr Austin mentions that he was one of the crew on her delivery passage from Fleetwood to Barry in 1911.

To quote his own words, 'She was a sister ship to the trawler *Louie Rigby*, then the fastest trawler in England. The *Kindly Light* was very fast but you had to understand her to be able to sail her correctly, otherwise she would soon have you over the tiller.'

He also recalled putting Lewis Alexander aboard fourteen ships in one week, thereby establishing an all-time record for a sailing pilot cutter. Also that the pilot's religious convictions did not allow him to be at sea on a Sunday.

Again, to quote Albert Austin's comments on the *Kindly Light*'s sailing qualities: 'The only fault with her was that you could not heave-to; she always liked the foresail amidships and the tiller lashed midships, and she would keep on sailing away as straight as a gun barrel.'

It was not usual for the pilots to take their wives to sea with them but on one occasion Lewis Alexander wished to attend a religious convention, with his wife, in Belfast. At the same time he hoped to bring back a ship from that port so, combining business with religious duty, he persuaded Mrs Alexander to take passage with him in the *Kindly Light*. This she agreed to do – but insisted on taking her featherbed with her for the voyage!

# CHAPTER EIGHT

# Wreck and Rescue

Though it was usual for a pilot to have his own cutter, sometimes a newly qualified man might share with another while waiting for his own boat, or possibly waiting delivery of a replacement. His crew would usually be one man as chief assistant, and a boy who could be either a youngster doing his pre-apprenticeship two years or an indentured apprentice doing the remaining five before going deep-sea for his Master's or mate's certificates, without which he could not become a pilot.

The pilot himself took very little hand in actually sailing the cutter, leaving this mainly to his man, known in the Bristol boats as a 'westernman' and in the Welsh as the 'man-in-the-boat', while the boy's job as well as rowing or sculling the pilot to or from the ships, was to do all the mundane 'domestic' chores, such as cooking, cleaning the lamps, polishing the brass and keeping the coal stoves going.

In the latter-day boats the pilot provided bedding and blankets, also basic provisions, cutlery and crockery, but in earlier times the man and the boy would have come aboard with their own 'donkey's breakfast' (straw-filled mattress), common practice in both coastwise and deep-water sailing vessels, and provide their own knife and fork, pannikin and drinking 'kid'. Again, in latter-day craft life-jackets were part of the boats' equipment but the hands provided their own clothing and oilskins in accordance with the current practice of the day.

A pilot boat obviously could not function with the usual sea-watches when on station, as everyone had a task to perform when a 'job' was on hand but sea-watches were observed when 'seeking' or passage making.

The standard of meals probably varied from boat to boat but in general the fare was fairly simple but plentiful, consisting of bread, cheap cuts of meat, vegetables and tea or cocoa backed up by sea-biscuits. Victualling a pilot boat with fresh meat and vegetables was no great problem as she was seldom at sea long enough for food to go bad.

Accommodation in the boats was divided into saloon and forecastle. The saloon bunks were occupied by the pilot on one side and man on the other, unless there were two pilots on board in which case the man shared the forecastle with the boy. Meals were taken together and usually prepared – and washed up – by the boy.

Pay varied over the years and from district to district but at the turn of the century it was the practice at Barry, for instance, to pay the men and apprentices a regular weekly wage, while the Bristol pilots paid on a share basis. A Barry apprentice in 1905 received 3s per week during his first year, 10s in the second, 17s 6d in the third and fourth and £1 in the fifth, while the Bristol pilots during the same period paid their westernmen 3s in the £ and the apprentice 'by arrangement'.

If this seems a pitifully small reward for a life of hard work, discomfort and danger, one should remember that the average ordinary seaman in a deep-water sailing ship received only £3 per month, while some were paid as little as £1 10s per month, so perhaps it was not too bad by the standards of the period.

Dismasting was not uncommon among the pilot craft, neither were collisions, both of which happened to the *Ellen* (No 15, Pilot J. Carey) when she was struck by the ss *Reginald* in the River Avon some time in 1899. The apprentice Charles Buck was drowned almost within sight of his home.

Similarly the Port Talbot cutter *Mary*, making port on a black night in a strong gale, took the wrong side of the breakwater and was lost. Strongly built and weatherly though they were, in the final analysis those cutters were at the mercy of the elements, having no auxiliary power to get them out of trouble in an emergency. True that the redoubtable Frank Trott had an auxiliary engine fitted in the *Marguerite* as early as 1908, but even then ethics forbade him to use it in competition with unpowered craft when 'seeking'. Built in 1893, one wonders if she would have survived into the 1990s without it.

The younger pilots, unlike some of an older generation, were always more than ready to employ innovations as they came along. Pilot Edwards of Barry, for instance, had his cutter, the *Frolic*, fitted with a tubular steel mainboom, presumably to obviate the boom breakage some times experienced when using patent roller reefing. This was revolutionary to say the least, as were the wire lanyards with which some of the Welsh boats were fitted. And no doubt if terylene sails and nylon rope had then been in existence, they, too, would have been used by the less conventional spirits.

Reverting to the subject of disaster at sea, Graham Farr writes of an occasion on 5 January 1826:

> . . . when the *Helen*, bound from the River Jade for Bristol, was boarded by the pilot and afterwards went missing in the Channel.[1] The probability of this type of trouble was naturally greatly increased when ships were boarded at a distance from home. Pilot Tom Thayer used to say that he once boarded a German barque off the Lizard and contrary winds blew them into the Bay of Biscay. It took him fifteen days to bring her to Bristol. On another occasion he was eleven days bringing a local barque from a position only ten miles west of Lundy.
>
> To end on a happier note, the Press of 1814 tells a tale of cool daring. It appears that the *Mary* (*Murphy*), bound from Newfoundland for Ross in

125

Ireland, had been captured off Cape Clear by the American privateer *Mammoth* and a prize crew put on board to take her to France. She was in the vicinity of Lundy when William Ray boarded her and found that the prize-master imagined himself in sight of islands off the French coast. History is silent as to whether Ray quickly disillusioned him or whether the first shock came when the prize crew heard Devon accents in Ilfracombe harbour, whither they were piloted.[2] Ray's skiff, incidently, was the *Britannia*, 20¾ tons, built at Ilfracombe in 1780.

One of the most spectacular disasters involving – albeit slightly – a Bristol Channel pilot boat, occurred when the battleship *Montagu* went ashore on the Island of Lundy on 30 May 1906.

The weather was thick with dense fog and a pilot boat was cruising in the vicinity of the island, with which she had been keeping in close touch. The 'man-in-the-boat' was on watch and was astonished to see a large man-o'-war loom up out of the murk to steer close to the cutter. As she drew abreast, she stopped engines and a voice hailed the pilot boat from the bridge, requesting the bearing and distance of Hartland Point. This was supplied immediately and correctly but the voice queried the answer and said that it must be wrong and that the pilot cutter must have lost her bearings. The battleship started her engines again and as she moved ahead the pilot boat shouted that if she kept on her present course she would be on the Shutter Rocks within ten minutes. Sure enough, in a short while, the unmistakable sounds of a large vessel going ashore came to the pilot boat through the fog. *HMS Montagu* was wrecked and so were the careers of some of her officers, who were convinced that they were on the rocks off Hartland.

Disasters also on occasion gave rise to incredible feats of bravery and seamanship, as in the case of John Morgan of the *Cardiffian*, whose rescue of the dismasted Barry cutter *Britannia* off the Morte Stone, has previously been mentioned. The *Britannia*, too, was subsequently to have her moment of glory, as commemorated in the following citation from the people of Barry to Pilot John Sparkes:

> To Mr John Sparkes, Master, Pilot Cutter No 18.
> Dear Sir,
>    We the undersigned, on behalf of the townspeople of Barry, beg your acceptance of this address and gift, as testifying to the civilized world an act of conspicuous bravery and the display of great courage in rescuing, under difficult circumstances and after persistent effort, three out of five survivors of the crew of the *ss Orianda* in the Bristol Channel on 11 February 1907. On a dark morning, in a heavy gale, you with your cutter *Britannia* bore down and picked up three men out of a water-logged

Bristol pilot skiff No.15 *Helen* after colliding with *s.s. Reginald* in the river Avon (Pilot J Carey), 1899. Apprentice Charles Buck was drowned in the accident. [courtesy PBA]

boat, when after two hours of extreme exposure, hope of rescue had almost disappeared. This, by no means the first time that the cry of 'distress' has prompted you to speedy and plucky action, has inspired these gifts as a token of the best feelings of mankind towards you for assisting your fellow men in an hour of danger, and we pray that Almighty God will abundantly bless you for having fulfilled the highest aim of all humanity, and that you will be favoured with long years and deserving prosperity.

Signed: *C. Milne* (Chairman), *J.A. Manaton, Sydney Davies, A.C. Clissett, W. Fowler, John George Wallihu, E. Griffiths, Geo. Wareham* (Treasurer), *H.J. Sanderson* (Hon Sec.), *J.B. Gratle.*

Another rescue involving a Pill hobbler took place a long way from the open sea – right up in the Avon Gorge, in fact. James Hazell was rowing under the Clifton Suspension Bridge at 5am on the morning of 18 September 1896 when he heard two heavy thuds in the water nearby. Rowing in the direction of the sound he discovered two children in the water, who had been thrown from the bridge by their father. They survived the ordeal of a 240ft drop into the icy, muddy Avon and became headline news in the city's newspapers. A photograph of Hazell, the two children and three policemen called to the scene appears in one of Reece Winstone's pictorial histories of the city.

It so happens that Hazell's father also figured in an episode that reads far more like fiction than known fact. In the early part of the nineteenth century he was picked up by the press gang and put on board the man-o'-war *Russell*, anchored in King Road. She sailed for Plymouth taking Hazell with her and leaving his distracted wife behind.

However, Mrs Hazell, a tailoress by trade, was a very determined lady. Sitting up night and day, she made a complete suit of naval clothes for herself, then walked to Plymouth from Pill to visit her husband on board the *Russell*. Beneath her own clothes she wore the sailor's rig-out she had made and once on board, dressed her husband in woman's clothes and sent him ashore, remaining on board in his place. She did a seaman's duty for ten days before giving away her identity! Meanwhile her husband walked back to Pill.

Pilots were supposed to have been exempt from the press gang but this rule was often violated, as in the case of Pilot Parfitt and four others who were seized and put on board the *Victory* just before Trafalgar. Parfitt died of wounds received in the famous battle as the *Victory* entered Plymouth.

Opposite Pill, on the other side of the river, was Myrtle Hall which, during the 1820s and 30s, was the home of the press gang commander. He employed as a servant a local girl called Nancy Carey of Crewkerne Pill, which was fortunate for the men of the village as Nancy, having eavesdropped on conferences, would warn likely victims so that the raids, when they took place, found the inns and taverns occupied only by the old men.

## NOTES

1. *Bristol Gazette*, 21 January 1826.
2. *Felix Farley's Bristol Journal*, 3 September 1814.

Pilot Frank Trott of the *Marguerite*. [courtesy R Denman]

# CHAPTER NINE

# Pilots' Pleasures

Life in the pilot cutters was not all toil and danger and it was the custom for the pilots to use their boats as holiday craft during summer time visits to the various Bristol Channel harbours. Ilfracombe was one of the most popular of these resorts, having a good paddle-steamer service from both sides of the Bristol Channel and also providing a safe haven with a flat, firm sandy beach where a boat could sit on her legs while running repairs and painting could be carried out and where she could be victualled and watered-up. Meanwhile the pilot could be with his family, whom he would have installed in one of the many lodging houses of the town and could take them out in his cutter for a day-sail when the weather was pleasant.

Ilfracombe also had other diversions to offer the men of the many sailing coasters (known to the pilots as 'Bideford Men-o'-War') and pilot craft which crowded the harbour in the days of sail. The Pier Hotel was the favourite venue for a sing-song and with beer at 2d a pint it did not take long for the men to get into good voice. Each pilot had his favourite song, such as 'The Volunteer Organist' and 'Creole Sue', which was 'Boss' Bennett's usual rendering, while Tom Morgan would contribute 'Honey, stay in your own Back Yard'. Apprentices, of course, were not – officially – allowed in a tavern but there was nothing to stop unindentured boys, denied beer, from drinking cider.

With drink so cheap, it is not surprising that some men allowed themselves to be taken over by it and oddly enough this frequently went hand-in-hand with a religious mania. One pilot recalls that, as an apprentice, he lived in terror of a 'man-in-the-boat' who would drink himself silly, a bottle in one hand and a Bible in the other. This man once chased him all over the cutter with murderous intent after the boy – left to sail the vessel single-handed in a strong wind, while the man went below to drink – had eased the main sheet an inch or two.

Another popular recreation for the pilots was racing. They loved to pit their craft against others for fun and each pilot-port would organise regattas, quite apart from the Annual Review Day races. It may seem surprising that men who raced against each other every working day for their living could derive pleasure from doing it for a pastime, but in fact they did and it was a matter of professional pride to do well in such races. And what an exhibition of superb seamanship it must have been, with every boat tuned to the limit and many specially rigged with extra long booms, extra large mainsails, huge jack-yard topsails and every man on board a highly skilled professional.

Retired Pilot R. Denman sailed in the *Marguerite* as apprentice with Frank Trott and remembers that Trott took to racing so seriously that he would take several weeks off during the regatta season in order to take part in as many races as possible. The *Marguerite* was put on the sand at Ilfracombe, scrubbed clean and her hull painted grey instead of the obligatory working black. Racing spars and sails were rigged and she then proceeded to win a string of victories all along the coast. Until recent years a brass plate was still mounted inside her main companion hatch, listing all her successes – including some events which Trott considered she had won but 'lost on a technicality'! He eventually sold the *Marguerite* and purchased the *Frolic*, which he worked and raced for the remainder of his career as a sailing pilot.

In 1936 the Barry Yacht Club organised a long-distance race within the Bristol Channel called 'The Cock o' the Bristol Channel' and the list of starters shows that no fewer than eight ex-Bristol Channel pilot cutters were taking part, including the *Frolic*, which by then had been a yacht in the Solent for many years.

Though seventy-nine years of age, her former owner, Frank Trott, needed little persuasion to skipper her round a gruelling course which took the boats well west of Lundy and kept them at sea for two full days. What is more, he sailed the *Frolic* home to victory, having kept the helm for forty-five hours continuously and beating, on handicap, a well-known yacht of the day, the *Zoraida*.

Built on pilot-cutter lines, the *Zoraida* was owned by Capt Franklin Ratsey of Cowes who, stung by his defeat, immediately challenged the *Frolic* to a private duel. Trott agreed without hesitation, the course this time being around Lundy Island. It was level pegging on the first leg during daylight but during the night the wily 79-year-old veteran piled on as much sail as he could carry and beat his rival fair and square. In his days as a working pilot he earned the reputation of being a hard man and old age had obviously not softened him!

Another retired Bristol Channel pilot pressed into service for that first 'Cock o' the Bristol Channel' race was so horrified at the way his old cutter had been cluttered up below decks since she had become a yacht that he insisted upon everything forward of the bitts and abaft the companion ladder being piled into the saloon, thereby rendering the bunks and settees unusable! The crew had to make the best of it while the old man, like Frank Trott, did most of the steering.

Some sixty years earlier, in 1875, there had been another famous private duel between the Newport pilot boat *J.N. Knapp* and Cardiff pilot Jonathan Lewis's *Anita*, crack ship of the Cardiff fleet at that time. The event provided a gala day and a paddle steamer was chartered as committee boat to anchor in Lundy Roads and serve as the weather mark. As the two contestants beat to the westward the weather deteriorated

Ex-pilot cutter
*Marguerite* as a yacht
under the burgee of the
Island Cruising Club of
Salcombe in the 1960s.
[courtesy John Corin]

Frank Trott's *Marguerite* rigged for racing. Note the bowsprit shroud 'whisker' booms, jack-yard topsail, large mainsail and running backstays, none of which were normal working rig.

until it was blowing a near gale, but both were sturdy craft with strong crews well able to cope with the prevailing conditions.

Lewis, however, was a somewhat cautious man and began to agitate to reduce sail, much to the disgust of his crew who were all experienced pilots in their own right. So they devised a plan to lure him below for a hot drink and when he fell for the stratagem they locked him in, held on to their canvas and won easily.

As Capt. Bartlett has recalled in Chapter Six, the highlight of the year in every pilot-port was 'Review Day', when all the pilot craft in port were inspected to ensure that every boat conformed to the rules as to lights, number of life-jackets, display of names, numbers etc. Many, as we now know, did not conform and as the august gentlemen of the committee passed through each boat – entering by the main companionway and leaving by way of the forehatch – essential gear was often passed quietly to the next boat in line so that the inspectors probably saw the same lot of equipment several times over. Inspection over, the boats would make sail and hoist their name pennants to the masthead for the ceremonial sail-past, terminating in a race which was closely followed by the committee boat – usually a paddle-steamer.

During the summer months it was usual to have carnival days with water-sports which included, of course, rowing and swimming races as well as greasy-pole competitions, and though Pill's present-day carnival is now called a 'Rag', it is still a recognisable continuation of the original concept. And there are still people alive in Pill who remember the old-style carnival days, when the participants were all 'local' to the district and all the fun was 'home-made'. Ashore there were processions led by the village band and there would be decorated horse-drawn floats.

The author does not, alas, remember those halcyon days but feels that he caught a glimpse of them just after the Second World War at Ilfracombe, before 'tourism' began to change the character of this once delightful little town. At that time there were still a few coasting ketches and schooners calling there and the crews of those in harbour on carnival day participated to the full, using their vessels as diving platforms, with spare spars rigged outboard for the greasy-pole, while the local fishermen loaned their pulling boats for rowing events. The procession ashore completed the scene and the whole atmosphere was one of uninhibited fun without any of the hooliganism from which so many such events suffer nowadays.

Not that the old pilot-ports were always shining temples of virtue. Drinking in the old days – as now – was a serious recreation for many and the number of public houses in Pill, for instance, was well out of proportion to its very small population. It is said, however, that for every pub, there was also a church, so perhaps the influence of the one helped to offset the other!

During the winter 'magic lantern' shows were a popular diversion ashore from the time of the first glass lantern slides in the latter half of the nineteenth century until the advent of the cinema proper in the early twentieth. Seamen's Missions and church

The *Marguerite*, launched in April, 1893 and here seen flying her winning flags at the opening of the Queen Alexandra Dock, Cardiff, in 1907. [courtesy R Denman]

halls were packed with local sea-going folk and their families on the night of a lantern show, for to people who seldom went out of their own neighbourhood for entertainment this was an advance of almost incredible sophistication. Most of the earliest slides were hand-drawn and strongly biblical in content but later ones were taken from photgraphic plates, and it is thanks to this that the pictorial records have survived, even though the original negatives have long since disappeared. So it is that a number of the pictures of working pilot boats reproduced in this book were taken from a lantern lecture of Pilot Lewis Alexander, who was a very popular giver of illustrated talks on the subject of his profession in and around Barry both during and long after his working lifetime.

# CHAPTER TEN

# The Revolt at Pill – and Amalgamation

In the days before the advent of the Welfare State a man's standard of living was directly proportionate to the work he was able to do. This was true of all seafarers but in the case of pilots, in particular, no ships meant no pay and this involved a degree of hardship for his family difficult to imagine in the Britain of today.

These conditions, on the other hand, bred tight-knit communities that would support each other to the last crust ashore in times of adversity, however great their rivalry at sea. Such a community was that of the pilot village of Crewkerne Pill, with its tough, turbulent people – sometimes quarrelling among themselves as small communities will do but turning a solid and belligerent front to any outsider who dared to interfere with their established way of life and showing short shrift to any of their number who proved disloyal.

Such an occasion arose in 1880, when the owners of the Bristol-based Great Western Steamship Co. decided to entrust the pilotage of their vessels to three selected pilots of Pill, to the exclusion of all others. At a time when that company commanded the bulk of Bristol's lucrative trans-Atlantic trade, this was a serious blow to the rest of the community which depended upon the prevailing system of free competition as a means of obtaining equal opportunities and, not unnaturally, it gave rise to bitter resentment against the privileged pilots.

At this time there were forty Bristol pilots and thirty-seven cutters, each manned by two westernmen and a boy (probably an apprentice) working out of Pill, so that the Great Western Steamship Company's arbitrary action – in direct contradiction to the recognised system – virtually condemned all but three selected pilots to near poverty. The compulsory pilotage area for the Port of Bristol began at Lundy and as the ships involved were large for their day, such as the ss *Cornwall*, *Somerset*, *Devon* and *Bristol*, each of 1,300 tons, and the *Dorset* of 1,500 tons, each was a potential source of a large proportion of a Bristol pilot's income.

The document which started all the trouble was a letter, dated 2 June 1880 from 'M.W. . . ., Great Western Steamship Company, to Mr R.C. . . . Pilot, Pill':

> Dear Sir, We have received no reply from the Docks Committee and
> therefore desire to make arrangements that either you or E- or G.R-

should always be in Lundy Roads when any of our boats are expected, so as to bring them up either to Bristol or Avonmouth.

If you have not already our private signal, we will provide you with one for each of your boats and will instruct our captains not to engage any other pilot unless neither of you happen to be down there. This, we hope, will never occur. Yours truly, pp MW-

From that moment the atmosphere of the village of Pill grew more and more tense and the attitude of the entire community towards the three privileged men became increasingly resentful. This showed itself for the first time in physical terms when one of the three was ambushed while walking home from Bristol one night by about twenty half-starved women, who tarred and feathered him. He probably got off lightly for whereas under normal circumstances he would have dropped down to Pill in the hobblers' boat, after docking the ship in the City Docks, he no doubt knew that to have followed the same practice just then was to have run the very real risk of being 'accidentally' drowned in the river. And after the tar and feathering incident, another pilot who had successfully solicited the Great Western line to join the selected three judiciously withdrew his application!

So the hostility grew and, one night just before Christmas, one of the 'non-selected' cutters lying in Lundy Roads hopefully spoke the Great Western Steamship Co's ss *Somerset*. As usual they were refused and the ship went to the cutter of one of the 'three'. The rejected pilot went below to take off his oilskins, leaving his westernman at the tiller with the cutter sailing very fast under double-reefed mainsail, foresail and jib. He came on deck again just in time to stop his man from ramming the rival boat by knocking him to the cockpit floor and putting the helm hard down, so that his cutter flew into the wind only a foot from the taffrail of the other. A moment more and nine men would have died that night in Lundy Roads. This was the measure of the desperation among the men who saw their livelihood being so unjustly denied them.

In January 1881 the strike of pilots' assistants began in earnest. The pilots themselves, being licensed under the corporation, could not refuse to work but at the same time could not operate without their westernmen. So, pushed to their limit, the latter took matters into their own hands. If they were not allowed to earn their living, they would make certain that the privileged three pilots would not do so either. High water was at 11.30am on that decisive morning and Pilots E- and C- got sail on their skiff preparatory to meeting two Great Western steamers. They sailed down the creek, only to find that a chain had been stretched across the entrance from a mooring post near the Custom House, the other end being taken by the women, boys, shopkeepers, publicans and others on the ferry slip side. The two pilots tried to sail the chain out, but without success.

That evening the town crier called a meeting at the parish rooms at 7pm to consider 'what steps shall be taken in the present crisis and God Save the Queen'.

The meeting was duly held and four propositions were made:

1   That no deep-sea skiff should be allowed to leave the creek;
2   That twenty of the younger pilots and forty westernmen should divide into watches of ten pilots and twenty westernmen on duty between the Holms and Bristol in the small yawls, to be relieved every twenty-four hours, to do all the piloting up and down until justice was done;
3   That the remaining pilots, westernmen and hobblers should divide into two watches of four hours to guard the creek during tide time and that any pilot, westernman or hobbler refusing to comply would be carried around the village on crossed poles with the word traitor pinned on his chest, a Union Jack on a pole in his hands and to be finally dumped in the 5ft pond at the head of the creek [this punishment was actually carried out in one case] and, finally;
4   That a treasurer be appointed and all monies put into a common fund to be shared out every Saturday at 11am.

Next morning Pilots C- and E- tried again to get out of the creek but the westernmen pulled two skiffs across the entrance. As reported in the *Post* of Thursday, 10 March 1881, Pilot C- actually drew a revolver when being attacked – and used it – until it was taken from him by the men, who then left him to the mercies of the women. They tarred and feathered both the pilot and his son and both suffered further injury before reaching home.

By this time the whole river and port were buzzing with the goings-on at Pill and the havenmaster, Capt Parsons RN, appeared on the scene to demand an explanation, resulting in a meeting that evening between the strike leaders and members of the City Council. The strike came to an end in about two months – the men having made their point – and out of it sprang the United Kingdom Pilots' Association, similar bodies later being formed in both the United States of America and Canada.

Once the dispute was settled, the pilots reverted to the previous system of individual competition and it was not until some thirty-seven years later that the amalgamation of Bristol pilots took place. A Cardiff pilot, James Duggan, is reputed to have pioneered this co-operative system of working, but it is unlikely that his influence extended as far west as Swansea, where the pilots amalgamated in 1898, or at Briton Ferry where amalgamation took place even earlier, in 1866.

To quote from the Cardiff Pilotage Authority's centenary booklet on the subject of amalgamation:

> In the year 1913 the Cardiff Pilotage Service underwent a great and important change. The high cost and waste involved with over sixty cutters cruising about the Channel seeking vessels requiring pilots

caused a majority of the pilots – only after long and considerable deliberations and much individual opposition – to adopt a scheme of amalgamation through the use of steam pilot cutters cruising at fixed pilot stations and with pilots working a rota system and pilotage dues earned divided equally among them. . . . There were three such stations – Nash Point, Barry Roads and Cardiff Roads.

One by one, however, all the pilotage districts adopted this system, Port Talbot in 1908, Cardiff in 1913, Barry in 1915, Newport in 1914, Gloucester/Sharpness in 1903 and Bristol in 1918. Thus ended the era of the independent sailing pilots and the great fleets of pilot cutters seeking far to the westward, and it is interesting to reflect that the Bristol pilot service, which is where it all started, was the last to forsake its sailing skiffs in favour of a steam cutter in 1922.

Upon Bristol's amalgamation in July 1918 the fleet of eighteen cutters was reduced to four, to work the stations, Nash Point, Barry Roads, Portishead and one boat in Barry Harbour to accommodate pilots arriving from Bristol with outward-bound ships. Each pilot would have a week at sea, a week at home to take outward-bound ships, and a week off duty unless urgently needed.

The Bristol pilotage district's area of operation had long since been contracted from distant Lundy Island, first back to the Holms and then to King Road, in the same way that the other pilotage districts established fixed stations. As ship-to-shore communication improved it was possible for a vessel to find her pilot at a predetermined position instead of the pilot seeking her.

One immediate effect of amalgamation was the redundancy of the great majority of the cutters. Almost overnight whole fleets of these splendid craft were laid up or put up for sale, except for the handful retained by the pilot companies as 'stand-by' boats. The Rowles-built skiffs, *Pet* and *E.M.C.*, were retained well into the 1930s, and the *Pet* was not finally sold off as a yacht until 1950.

Not surprisingly, discerning yachtsmen soon snapped up the best of them, one of the first being John R. Muir, author of the book *Messing About In Boats*, who bought, in turn, the Newport cutter *Maud* (renamed *Saladin*) the *Britannia* of Barry (which had figured in at least two spectacular sea rescues, once as the victim and once as the rescuer), and the Bristolman, *Freda*. Others sold off at give-away prices included the *Marguerite* (whose name now has a 'T' added), the *Alpha*, the *Faith*, the *Sea Breeze*, the *Cariad*, the *Mascotte*, the *Kindly Light* (renamed the *Theodora*), the *Olga*, the *Wave* (renamed the *Peggy*), the *Rene B* (renamed the *Raider*) the *Breeze* and the *Madcap*, to name but a few that have survived into the 1990s.

There must be many more scattered all over the world, for a pilot cutter in good condition could go anywhere and sometimes one comes across one among a gaggle of miscellaneous craft in odd corners of old docks, often much converted but still recognisable for what she was. For, wherever they are, they stand out from everything else around them, carrying a distinction that no pleasure yacht could ever acquire. On one occasion I was looking down upon the yacht harbour from the top of the Rock of Gibraltar and there, among the glassfibre playthings was, unmistakably, a pilot cutter. Losing no time in getting down there, I was delighted to find the old *Rene B* of Barry, then known as the *Raider*.

Some boats were bought to continue working, such as the *Fanny Saunders* of the Barry/Newport service, which was converted to a trading smack to carry sand or coal between Lydney and Oldbury Pill in the River Severn. Many others were already old when they were laid up and died as rotting hulks in creeks and mudbanks up and down the Bristol Channel.

It is impossible to say exactly how many exist today, in the late 1990s, but Lloyds Register of Yachts lists fifteen still in sailing commission and there are many more unlisted and some being used as house-boats.

Fortunately, two cutters have been purchased for preservation and restoration as examples of their type. Lewis Alexander's *Kindly Light* has been aquired by a private owner while a syndicate has the well-known *Cariad*, built for the Cardiff fleet by Rowles of Pill in 1904, and with the distinction of being literally the last sailing pilot cutter to work under sail in the Bristol Channel. In December 1922, as Bristol skiff No 2, she handed over her station to the new steam cutter *Queen Mother* and hauled down for the last time the red and white pilot flag that she and her sisters had worn so proudly for so long.

And with her went the last days of the sailing pilots and their magnificent cutters. Never again would a homeward-bound ship find a Bristol Channel pilot cutter far out in the Atlantic, fighting wind and weather to be the 'western' boat and first to speak her. Never again would one be found sheltering under Lundy in a full gale or 'Round the Land', sitting on her own reflection in a flat, frustrating calm while her quarry passed her by outside hailing distance.

The Bristol *Queen Mother* was especially adapted from her previous occupation as a Lowestoft steam drifter, having been built as such in 1916 by Colby Bros. of Oulton Broad for W.A.W. Greaves of Lowestoft. In 1917 she was requisitioned by the Admiralty for War Service as a submarine net drifter until, in September 1919, she was returned to her original owners, who eventually sold her on to the newly formed Bristol Channel Steam Pilot Cutter Company Ltd. She was converted for pilotage work by P.K. Harris of Appledore.

According to my good friend Pilot John Rich her motion at sea could be likened to one of the more sick-making rides on a fair-ground! In this she was akin to the earlier Welsh steam cutters which were beautiful to look at, with yacht-like, graceful lines such as the Cardiff *W.W. Jones* and the *Edmund Hancock*, with bright varnish and gleaming brasswork to keep the boys busy, but were uncomfortable in anything of a

The *Cariad* as a working boat.

The *Cariad*, built by E. Rowles of Pill in 1904 and the last sailing cutter in full time service in the Bristol Channel. She handed over her station to the steam cutter *Queen Mother* in December, 1922. [courtesy John Corin]

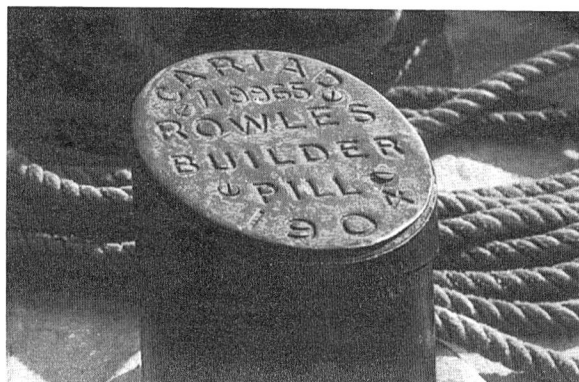

The *Cariad*'s rudder-head builder's plate. [courtesy John Corin]

sea, and were eventually replaced by the less attractive but more suitable vessels such as the *Chimera* and the *Ilona*.

From these have developed the present-day, fast and powerful diesel cutters capable of boarding, or taking off a pilot in almost any weather and with a minimum of expensive delay. Nowadays the pilot waits ashore in a warm and comfortable lodge near the dock entrance – a far cry from the hard conditions endured by his sailing predecessor. Nevertheless, a modern pilot is his worthy successor, carrying out a task which is in many ways more demanding, and handling ships of vastly greater tonnage and technical complexity than his predecessors could have dreamed of. Moreover, there is not one who is not proud to be carrying on the traditions established by the old sailing pilots and their fine boats, whose epitaph must be the words of Commander Muir's old pilot hand: 'Heave-to! You don't heave-to in *them* ships unless you're waiting for something!'

# APPENDIX 1

## Bristol Channel Pilotage Acts (Newport), 1807–1921

## The Act of 1807

'An Act for ascertaining and establishing the Rates of Wharfage, Cannage, Plankage, Anchorage and Moorings to be received at the lawful Quays in the Port of Bristol, for the Regulation of the Crane Keepers in the said Port, and for the better regulation of Pilots and Pilotage of Vessels navigating the Bristol Channel, 1807.

All Vessels sailing, navigating, or passing up, down, or upon the Bristol Channel to the Eastward of Lundy Island, excepting Coasting Vessels and Irish Traders, should be piloted, conducted, and navigated by Pilots duly authorised and licensed by the Mayor, Burgesses, and Commonalty of the City of Bristol by Warrent under their Corporate Seal. Masters who failed to do so forfeited Double the Pilotage Fee, plus five pounds for every fifty tons burthen of such ship.'

This Act merely confirmed what had been the practice from time out of mind, but as other Channel ports became larger, it caused great dissatisfaction and indeed, following a Government Commissioners' Inquiry at Newport in 1833, we read a complaint that:

> There is no power to appoint Pilots: the consequence is that many persons take on themselves the office for which they are unfit. When Vessels from foreign ports take Pilots, and they are brought to the Harbour in safety, the Bristol Pilots demand exorbitant fees, which the Masters of such vessels are obliged to pay.

## The Act of 1836

The first Newport Harbour Act 1836, took advantage of an earlier act 'for the Amendment of the Law respecting Pilots and Pilotage and also for the better preservation of Floating Lights and Beacons' passed in 1826, and empowered the Corporation of Trinity House to license Pilots for Newport. The Trinity House appointed three residents of Newport, who were called Sub-Commissioners of Pilotage for the Port of Newport. These gentlemen examined the qualifications of candidates and on their satisfactory Certificate, the Trinity House gave a licence to the Pilot. Thereafter, with certain exemptions, 'all vessels sailing, navigating, or passing into, out of, or within the Port of Newport were conducted and piloted by such pilots only as shall be licensed by the Trinity House, and by no other Pilots or Person whomsoever.'

## The Penarth Act of 1857

It is noteworthy that by the Penarth Harbour, Dock and Railway Act of 1857, a separate system of Pilotage for Penarth was also authorised and it seems likely that a deal of dissatisfaction was being manifested in other Channel ports, because in the year 1861 a Bill was before Parliament, 'Whereas owing to the great Extension of Trade in the several ports of Cardiff, Newport and Gloucester since the passing of the 1807 Act, it is expedient that a separate system of Pilotage should be established in the Bristol Channel in connection with those respective ports, under the Supervision of Local Boards for each of such Ports.'

## The Acts of 1861–1913

The Newport Corporation, with the full support of the Harbour Commissioners, fought this Bill and even promoted their own Bill for Abolishing Compulsory Pilotage in the Bristol Channel. This resulted in the Compulsory Pilot clauses in the original Bill, and so the Bristol Channel Pilotage Act 1861 was enacted.

On 9 November 1861, the Newport Pilotage Authority was born, consisting of the Mayor for the time being, three persons who were appointed by the mayor, Aldermen and Burgesses of the Borough of Newport, three persons by the Newport Harbour Commissioners and one person by the Newport Dock Company.

The District over which this Board had jurisdiction was 'That portion of the Bristol Channel which lies Eastward of Lundy Island up to and including King Road, and the River Usk as far as Caerleon.'

The original Board was augmented under the Alexandra (Newport) Dock Act 1876 and the Pilotage Orders Confirmation Act 1893.

This Authority, together with the other Bristol Channel pilotage authorities, appears to have worked much better than in other districts in the United Kingdom, where conditions were chaotic, necessitating the passing of the Merchant Shipping (Exemption from Pilotage) Act 1897, for instance, and the Government made a real effort to improve the diverse and various pilotage organisations by enacting the Pilotage Act 1913, wherein the Board of Trade was empowered to make Pilotage Orders for districts where it thought it expedient, and to establish new and define the limits of pilotage districts etc.

# The Act of 1921

Whether or not the Great War 1914–18 delayed matters, it was not until the year 1921 that Newport received attention and under Pilotage Orders Confirmation (No 5) Act 1921, the Newport Pilotage Order was enacted and came into force on 19 August 1921, repealing the Bristol Channel Pilotage Act 1861, so far as it relates to the Pilotage District Sec: 7 of the Alexandra (Newport) Dock Act 1876 and the Pilotage Orders Act 1893, so far as it relates to the Pilotage District.

## Constitution of the Authority

The constitution of the Authority was and remains:

- Three members appointed by Newport County Borough Council.
- Two members appointed by the Alexandra Docks (B.T.C.).
- Three members appointed by Newport Harbour Commissioners.
- Three Shipowners' representatives appointed by Newport Shipowners' Association, and if that body ceases to be fairly representative of shipowners using this Port, then by such body or bodies nominated for the purpose by the Ministry of Transport.
- Three members elected by the licensed pilots from past or present pilots with two 'stand-in' substitutes.

## Pilotage District Boundaries

The Pilotage District is defined to be the waters of the Bristol Channel bounded seawards by an imaginary line from Hartland Point Lighthouse to Lundy Island South Lighthouse, thence thro' Caldy Island Lighthouse to the Mainland, and landwards by an imaginary straight line from Goldcliff Point to Clevedon Pierhead Light, but excluding all Docks (but not any entrance basin or Lock leading thereto) and also excluding ports lying within Trinity House Outport Districts.

The seaward boundary is common to all eight Channel pilotage authorities, the landward boundaries are adjusted to suit the different Authorities, but Newport, Cardiff and Barry all have the same Goldcliff-Clevedon boundary. Eastward of this line comes within the Districts of Bristol and Gloucester Pilotage Authorities and pilotage becomes compulsory.

With the exception of passenger-carrying ships, as provided by Section II of the 1913 Act and the above, there is no other compulsory pilotage in the Bristol Channel.

A pilot's licence granted by Barry Pilotage Authority entitles the holder to pilot vessels to Barry and Barry Roads only when such vessel is bound for Barry Docks, but with this exception, other pilots of all other Authorities can pilot vessels to any port which lies within their District. HOWEVER provision is made in the Orders that where a ship is bound for a port, and the pilot is licensed by another Authority, he shall be superseded by a pilot belonging to that port on offering his services and the pilotage rates shall be divided between the two pilots in such proportion as may in case of dispute be determined by the Authority.

## Extension of Newport Pilotage District to Eastward

It will be seen that on the Monmouthshire coast, the area to the east of Goldcliff, which is also the eastern Harbour boundary, lies within the concurrent jurisdiction of Bristol and Gloucester Pilotage Authorities and pilotage is compulsory.

Whilst the various Pills on the coast between Goldcliff and Chepstow have been used by vessels since the earliest times, it is doubtful if any foreign-going vessel ever used them and if so, they would be piloted by pilots licensed by Bristol City. It must not be forgotten that Gloucester pilots are stationed at Barry (on the Cardiff cutter) by arrangement, when ships are expected for Sharpness. Consequently they also would have a good case in the event of a commercial wharf or port being constructed eastward of Goldcliff. As pilotage eastward of Goldcliff is confined to the Bristol side of the Welsh Grounds, it is considered that Newport's case would be strongest. However, in the event of such a commercial venture, leading to a dispute between authorities, Trinity House could make it Their Outport.

The above is extracted, by permission, from documents in the Newport, Monmouthshire, Library.

The ex-Cardiff pilot yawl *Breeze*, as a yacht in 1948, built by John Cooper of Pill in 1887 and the only known transom stern survivor from his yard.

# APPENDIX 2

## Bristol Channel Pilot Cutters
### The Survivors – At 1999

Whenever I come across one of the vast marinas which have sprung up all around our coasts I always – almost subconsciously – cast an eye over the mass of metal masts, with their incessant cacophony of jangling, tapping halliards – the 'old fashioned' ones, that is. The 'modern' ones have halliards led inside the masts – and occasionally I see what I have been hoping for – the wooden mast of an old-timer, rigged as for gaff and boom. Usually she proves to be a nice old wooden yacht, an echo of pre high-tech sailing days. Sometimes the top hamper tells me that she is something more interesting – an ex-working boat. Even better is an ex-Bristol Channel pilot cutter, one of a surprising number still in commission. Surprising in that the last one built for the Bristol Channel pilot service is now some 88 years old.

With its world-wide reputation as a strong and powerful sea-boat, the Bristol Channel pilot cutter is probably the yardstick by which most other similar types are measured. The fact that I have compiled a list of seventeen known survivors, either in full sailing commission, or as exhibits in two or three museums, is proof of their durability. There are almost certainly others scattered around the world for they are renowned globe-trotters.

The oldest, and still one of the smartest boats on my list, is *Madcap*, built by Davies & Plain at Cardiff in 1875. She is still in excellent sailing condition after 124 years. As a Welsh pilot yawl (as the Welsh called their cutters), she was worked hard, but, according to my records, was only in serious trouble once, when she went ashore at Clevedon in 1902.

Twelve years after the launch of *Madcap*, John Cooper of Pill on the River Avon, produced the *Breeze* for Pilot Cope, another Welsh pilot. She is, I believe, the only surviving example of Cooper's transom-sterned type. Just after the Second World War, her then owner inaugurated the 'Breeze Cup' Race, between Barry and Porlock Weir – her home port at that time. Apart from having been painted white, she was unchanged from her pilot days, and I shall never forget what an evocative sight she made as we followed her across, sailing hard with a quartering wind against the magnificent back drop of the Exmoor coastline, in the warm light of a late summer's evening – much as she must have looked a hundred times when bound out 'seeking to the westward'.

She then went through a period of neglect at Porlock Weir, and was all but written off, until a Barry Yacht Club member rescued her, towing her back to Barry held

The *Breeze* at Porlock Weir. Built by Cooper of Pill in 1887.

together internally by chains stretched between her frames! He made such a splendid job of renovating her that Barry Yacht Club presented him with a special trophy in recognition of his achievement. She now lives once again at Porlock Weir, and should be good for another 100 years.

In 1889 Hambly of Cardiff built the *Marion*, for Pilot John Morse. Her hull form, 'cod's head and mackerel tail', was rather advanced for the time with a very pleasing spoon bow, cut-away forefoot and a sweet run. Following her pilot service she continued to be owned in Cardiff. One pre-war photograph shows her as a very stylish yacht named *Colaba*. Post-war she eventually became the property of a very dedicated young man in Dorset who lavished his limited resources and many hours of hard manual work on her until circumstances forced him to part with her. However, his dedication kept her alive until she was taken over by an enthusiast who was able to complete the work very thoroughly indeed. Not a very experienced sailing man, he had the good sense to ask, and to follow, the advice of experts in wooden boats, incuding one man who had rebuilt his own pilot cutter. The result was a superbly restored boat which was re-launched with all due ceremony, champagne and all.

The year 1893 saw the building of the *Marguerite*, thought by many to have been 'Cracker' Rowles' masterpiece. In the hands of Pilot Frank Trott, a double licence pilot for both Cardiff and Barry, she soon made a name for herself as a very fast boat indeed, proving formidable to her professional rivals when seeking, and a frequent winner of the pilot boat races. In fact Trott was a racing fanatic. So much so that, at the beginning of the 'regatta' season, he would take the *Marguerite* down Channel, put her up on a beach, clean and repaint her bottom, paint the hull a non-regulation grey, and sail around the coast competing in – and often winning – all the races he could get to, returning to full-time piloting at the end of the season. It appears, however, that he was not a goood loser, judging by the engraved brass plate on the forward ledge of the main hatch, inscribed with his victories. One read, rather sourly, 'disqualified upon a technical point'.

Regrettably the brass plate, which had survived for sixty years or more, was stolen, but his collection of trophies could at one time be seen at the Pilotage Office. Trott was evidently a man with an eye to the future when he had an engine fitted to the *Marguerite* in 1908, but he would not have been allowed to use this when he was working.

The *Marguerite* has been fortunate in her owners since her working days, including a spell on loan to the Island Cruising Club of Salcombe, and is now owned, or at least used, in the West Indies, once again sporting her grey and black colour scheme on an extensively rebuilt hull. In this guise she made minor maritime history during the August of 1998, when she put out from Halifax, Nova Scotia, with a Halifax pilot for the famous Cunard liner *Queen Elizabeth 2*. This was the first time for nearly eighty years that a Bristol Channel pilot cutter had performed this service.

The *Solway*, now known as *Carlotta*, was built for a Welsh pilot by W.H. Halford of Gloucester in 1900. I know very little of her recent past, but she was a well-known yacht before the Second World War, and now resides in Vancouver, Canada – so the Atlantic was obviously no problem for her.

*Baroque* is another well travelled vessel, having belonged at one time to the intrepid Major H.W. Tilman who cruised extensively to both the Arctic and Antarctic, and who had previously had the misfortune to lose the well-known Cardiff yawl *Mischief*, and also the Newport pilot vessel *Sea Breeze* in the ice. Fortunately, the *Baroque* did not share their fate, and remains today the fine cutter she was when launched by Hambly of Cardiff in 1902. It may be remembered that she featured in the BBC television series *Under Sail*, and was filmed sailing on the Dutch waterways. When I asked why she was not filmed at sea, they told me it was because it was too rough out there. The ghost of her old pilot must have had a chuckle at that!

For some years the *Alpha*, built by Liver & Wilding of Fleetwood in 1904 for Pilot Sam Davies, held a reputation for speed. She had been built on trawler lines and was therefore somewhat different in hull form to the Westcountry boats. Until recently her devoted owner of many years had kept her in immaculate condition, but ill health finally compelled him to part with her. Imagine his feelings when he learned that in the hands of her new owner, she had fallen over, sustaining serious damage. Enough, it was thought, to put her out of action for good. Not so. To my great delight she magically appeared in Bristol City Docks in early December 1991, looking absolutely superb – externally at least. There was still work to be done below decks which would take some months to complete, but her new owners have worked a minor miracle in her rebuilding.

One extensively rebuilt cutter that *did* get to sea again is the ex-Bristol skiff *Wave*, now known as the *Peggy*. She was built by Rowles of Pill in 1903 and worked by Richard Case from 1903 to 1907 as Bristol No. 10. Having been turned down by Bristol City Museum as a potential floating exhibit, she was eventually acquired by Diccon Pridie of Bristol in the 1980s. Diccon and his wife, with additional help from friends, have done a splendid job on her, and she now regularly graces the waters of the Bristol Channel she was built for. Whilst chipping out the concrete from between the floors, they found that the 'hardcore' at each end consisted of the old fashioned 'dimple-necked' lemonade bottles, thus confirming the old pilot's rule of 'keeping the ends light'! The *Peggy*, too, had her moment of glory when she starred in the HTV's series *Coastline*, with the author a willing participant aboard.

*Cariad* is a vessel of considerable note, having been owned for many years by the distinguished marine historian and author, the late and much lamented Frank Carr, whose voyages in her have become a part of yachting history. *Cariad* was yet another Rowles creation of 1904, this time being built for the Welsh pilots, Davies and Jones. After the Welsh pilots' amalgamation she was sold to Bristol as Pilot No. 2, with Pilot

Enoch Watkins of Pill as her new owner. The Bristol pilots did not finally abandon sail for steam until as late as 1922, and in December of that year, *Cariad* claimed the unique distinction of being the very last sailing pilot cutter in the Bristol Channel to keep her station under sail. She lowered her pilot flag for the last time on 7th December, handing over to the steam cutter *Queen Mother*, on whose deck was 'Cracker' Rowles himself, to witness the occasion. The end of an era and a very poignant moment that must have been. During the 1970s the *Cariad* was put in the care of the International Sailing Craft Association's Exeter Maritime Museum, where some restoration work was started. Then in the late 1980s she went to Newport where the Newport Maritime Trust had hoped to complete the job and to put her on show. Unfortunately this did not work out, and she is now owned by a Bristol-based syndicate. *Cariad* is very special in the history of her type and no effort must be spared to save her.

One of the best restorations of recent years has been that of the big ex-Newport cutter *Mascotte*. She was built and worked by Pilot T. Cox of Newport in 1904. During the 1960s I went on board her in Whitewall Creek on the River Medway, where she was being used as a houseboat by a dedicated couple who were fighting the all-too-familiar battle to get her to sea again. Unfortunately the battle was lost and they had to part with her. The next time I saw her, this time on the south coast, history seemed to be repeating itself. I am always sad to see these wonderful people, who have the courage to take on these big old boats, thwarted after putting in so much effort, and it can be very little consolation for them to realise that they have been keeping the job alive for someone else to finish. That is what happened with the *Mascotte* when she was taken over by a new owner, who was able to do the work she so desperately needed. New stem, counter and frames. In fact a re-build. The result is absolutely superb and one of the finest examples of a pilot cutter in full sailing commission to be seen at the present time.

The *Frolic* was one of the relatively few Bristol Channel pilot craft to have been built 'over the (Bideford) Bar'. She was the work of Westacott, at Cleave, North Devon in 1905, and was quite revolutionary in several respects. Firstly she was built to drawings instead of the usual half-model and the designer was C. Hancock. Secondly she was built to act in a dual capacity – as a pilot boat and as a yacht for chartering purposes, which, no doubt, accounts for her having an owner's stateroom. Thirdly she was fitted with a tubular steel main boom, probably to reduce the possibility of a broken boom when gybing with a well reefed mainsail. Her hull form was also unconventional for her day, having an almost straight stem as far as the cut-water, then cut back sharply at an angle to her full depth about one third of her length. She also had steeply cambered decks, which, so one old pilot hand told me, were not at all popular among the men sailing the boat. It is interesting that the famous Frank Trott purchased *Frolic* to replace the *Marguerite*. No doubt her innovations appealed to his competitive spirit. I last saw the *Frolic* many years ago near Mylor, and was surprised to find her schooner-rigged. My latest information is that she is now abroad.

A museum which has a pilot cutter in good condition is Swansea. The magnificent *Olga* found a good home there in 1984 and now graces the collection of floating exhibits alongside the museum building. She was built 'round land' by J. Bowden of Porthleven in 1909 for Harry Edmunds of Barry who was, I think, the last Bristol Channel pilot alive who had owned and worked his own cutter. I tried to interview him in the 1960s but to my regret he was too frail to handle it. The *Olga* worked as a fishing boat in the 1920s and the museum has a good photograph of her at that time, with her fishing number superimposed upon her original 'By' (Barry Pilots) pilot marking on her mainsail.

There were two main builders of pilot boats in Porthleven, namely Bowden and Kitto, sharing equally the fine reputation of Porthleven-built craft. It was Kitto who, in 1910, built the *Rene B*, now known as the *Raider*, for George Bennett of Barry. In common with her sisters, her post-piloting career has been varied. I remember her as the mother-ship to a sailing school in the River Yealm, after which she was owned abroad in the Mediterranean. After that she became a virtual hulk in Ireland, but was rescued just in time by an American friend. He shipped her out to New England, and has almost completed a most beautiful restoration job on her, which has taken him eleven years so far.

Another Cornish yard, that of Slade of Fowey, was responsible for the *Cornubia*, in 1911, at the order of Barry pilot, George Morris. He could never have foreseen that over eighty years later his yawl would still be in existence as the yacht *Hirta*, with thousands of sea miles to her credit. Sadly, she is at the time of writing laid up at Gweek in Cornwall, her future uncertain.

The *Kindly Light* was built by Armour Brothers of Fleetwood, also in 1911. Lewis Alexander was impressed with the Fleetwod-built *Alpha*, and decided to go there for his own new boat – but not to the same yard. Apparently he had heard that the foreman shipwright at Messrs. Liver & Wilding had moved over to Armour Brothers. Hence the similarities beween the two boats. The *Kindly Light* was named *Theodora* after her working days were over, and kept in regular commission as a yacht and youth training vessel, until the newly formed Maritime Trust acquired her as an example of her type. In due course she was placed in the care of Cardiff Industrial Museum, which, in my opinion, ill-advisedly put her in a small out-door dry-dock – the worst possible thing to do to an old wooden boat – at the mercy of every kind of weather, from hard frost to blazing sunshine. It would have been better to have kept her afloat, and better still to have kept her sailing. If this was not practicable, she should have been placed inside a building, with carefully monitored temperature and humidity control. Otherwise her timbers just rot, or dry out, until the structure just falls apart.

Pilot yawl *Olga*, Gloucester Dock, August 1995. Drawing by author.

The *Letty*, built in 1906, and restored in 1996.

The *Letty* as the fishing boat *Roaming* at Arklow.

Fortunately she has been rescued by an enthusiast who is doing an extensive restoration job on her, under the watchful eye of Norman Alexander – son of her original pilot/owner Lewis.

Finally there is one survivor whose identity is demanding quite a lot of detective work. She is without doubt a Rowles-built skiff, but had been used as a fishing boat for many years, named *Roaming*, out of Arklow, Ireland, until being taken to north Wales to become a cutter-rigged yacht. All the available evidence points to her being the Bristol skiff *Letty* of 1905, which was known to have left Pill to become a fishing boat in 1918. I came across her at Arklow and was told that she was indeed an ex-Bristol Channel pilot cutter, and had been there for many years, but that no one could remember her original name. Unfortunately she had been stripped of all her original fittings above and below decks, leaving no identifiable features which might have 'pinned her down'. The investigation continued and thanks to diligent research by retired Bristol Channel pilot John Rich, it has now been established beyond all reasonable doubt that she is the Pill skiff *Letty*, built for and worked by his grandfather, Pilot Arthur James Gilmore-Dickens from 1906. She is now a fully restored sailing cutter under her original name. This then is the list of the known examples remaining of a fleet which once numbered into three figures. I would be grateful to be told of any others I have not caught up with as there could well be one or more ex-Bristol Channel pilot boats waiting to be re-discovered somewhere in the world, for as we have seen these vessels were eminently sea-worthy and ventured widely in their latter days.

In 1996 the Bristol Channel Pilot Boat Owners Association was formed for the historical research of these boats, exchange of experience and expertise of their restoration and repair and the revival of the Pilot Boat Races in which they regularly competed in their working days. Most of them are now well over 90 years old and it is a thrilling experience to see these venerable rivals battling it out on the same waters on which they sailed so long ago.

The qualification for full membership of the Association is ownership of a sailing boat known to have been registered as a pilot craft working out of a Bristol Channel port. Other enthusiasts are welcome as associate members.

# APPENDIX 3

## Museums and Models

Although the *Cariad* can claim the distinction of handing over the role of full-time station-keeping sailing cutters to steam, this did not mean that they disappeared instantly from the Bristol pilot service. At least three survived into the early 1950s, namely the *Bertie* and the *Berkeley Castle* as cut down accommodation hulks at Portishead and the fully rigged *Pet* as a relief boat, first at Pill and then in Bristol City Dock. The latter was sold out of the pilot service in about 1950 or 51, to Pilot Seymour Ellis whose family had worked her since her building by Rowles in 1905. He gave her a coat of white paint and cruised in her for a season or two, then sold her on to the first of a series of owners who seemed to have insufficient funds or knowledge to keep her up together. For some time she was used as a houseboat by students, during which time the author of this book went aboard and noticed that below deck she seemed to be in reasonable condition but nothing above deck was being done to maintain any of the sailing gear.

After the students left her she was occupied only spasmodically and eventually deserted altogether and it was heart-breaking to see this fine, powerful vessel – a superb example of her type – crumbling away almost before one's eyes. At last the author could stand it no longer so, lacking the means to rescue her himself, approached the Bristol City Museum with the suggestion that the *Pet* should be acquired by them and restored for display to the public. Sadly, such thinking was too radical for Bristol at that time so she was allowed to deteriorate to the point where she became a liability, being condemned finally to be broken up at the Underfall Yard in 1963.

However, the seed had been sown and in due time the museum authorities invited your author to help in selecting a suitable pilot cutter for preservation! The first candidate was the *Peggy* (ex-*Wave*) which was currently on the market but the surveyor's report was unfavourable, so she was dropped. Ironically she was subsequently bought by a private individual who put her back into full sailing commission.

A second attempt was made with the legendary *Marguerite*, at that time based in Salcombe. During the inspection the opportunity was taken to take off her lines and to make accurate sketches of the accommodation, which was largely unchanged from her working days. Hence the cut-away drawing which appears elsewhere in this book. Sadly, she too was condemned by the surveyor but like the *Peggy*, she too survived into the 1990s to make long voyages including trans-Atlantic.

The Bristol skiff *Pet* just after being taken out of service c.1950.

The *Pet* just before being broken up c.1960.

Another view of the *Pet* in her last days.

The museum then abandoned any ideas for preserving a genuine full-scale cutter and opted instead for an accurate model. This was eventually built by Bassett-Lowke, whose modelling excellence is world-renowned. It casts no reflection on them that, having been fed inaccurate information, some details had to be corrected by the Bristol model-maker and marine historian, the late Norman Poole before it could be put on display.

Cardiff Museum also has two pilot boat models, namely the *Hope* cutter and a Swansea Bay pilot schooner but when Cardiff Industrial Museum came into being they went one better and aquired the genuine pilot yawl the *Kindly Light* from the Maritime Trust. Unfortunately, as mentioned in an earlier chapter, they made the mistake of putting her ashore in a small dry dock, where she was allowed to dry out and was seldom 'aired through'. Thus she began to rot and was saved in the nick of time by an enthusiast who purchased her and undertook the task of completely re-building this lovely old boat.

Following the example of Bristol, Cardiff commissioned from Kelvin Thatcher of Norfolk a very large model of the Welsh yawl *Marguerite* for show-case display. At a scale of 1":1ft. she is most impressive.

The historic *Cariad* is another pilot cutter which suffered from museum neglect – albeit inadvertently. Under-funded and short of skilled labour, most provincial museums are just not equipped for the care of old wooden boats, which should either be kept afloat and if possible, sailed, or displayed under cover in temperature and humidity controlled conditions. Otherwise they fall apart. Fortunately, as in the case of the *Kindly Light*, a group of skilled enthusiasts have taken her over – we hope in time to save her.

A museum which really does look after its floating exhibits is Swansea, where they have a pilot cutter in magnificent condition. She is the *Olga*, built by J. Bowden at Porthleven in 1909, and is sailed regularly as a competitor in the Annual Pilot Cutter Race, revived by the Pilot Boat Owners Association after a lapse of some fifty years.

Failing the real thing, a good and well researched model can be both decorative and instructive and since the initial publication of this book, the Bristol Channel pilot cutter has caught the imagination of modellers the world over. Many model-sailing lakes can now display a veritable fleet of *Marguerites*, *Cariads* and *Hildas* most of which, when not sailing, make very handsome display models such as, for instance, the ¾":1ft *Marguerite* by Christopher West of Bristol, which won the Gold Medal award at the International Model Engineering Exhibition, Olympia in 1993. In the water this model looks the 'real thing' but with its false keel removed and on its display stand it would do credit to any maritime museum in the world.

It is interesting that some of the present-day Bristol Channel pilots are interested in models of the craft worked by their ancestors, either commissioning them or, as in the case of retired pilot Syd Dickens, enjoy modelling not only the popular ones but also researching those of a much earlier period than those sailed by his own forebears, such as the skiff *Trial* of 1847.

Malcolm Darch of Salcombe, South Devon, must rank among the top flight of showcase-model builders in the country. Having trained and worked as a wood-building shipwright in one of our most prestigious yacht yards, he now employs his skills in miniature scale to produce the most exquisite model sailing craft to be seen anywhere. One of his best is a 1/36th to scale model of the *Marguerite*. Resulting from meticulous research it is perfect in every detail.

The *Marguerite*, built for Bristol City Museum by Basset-Lowke.

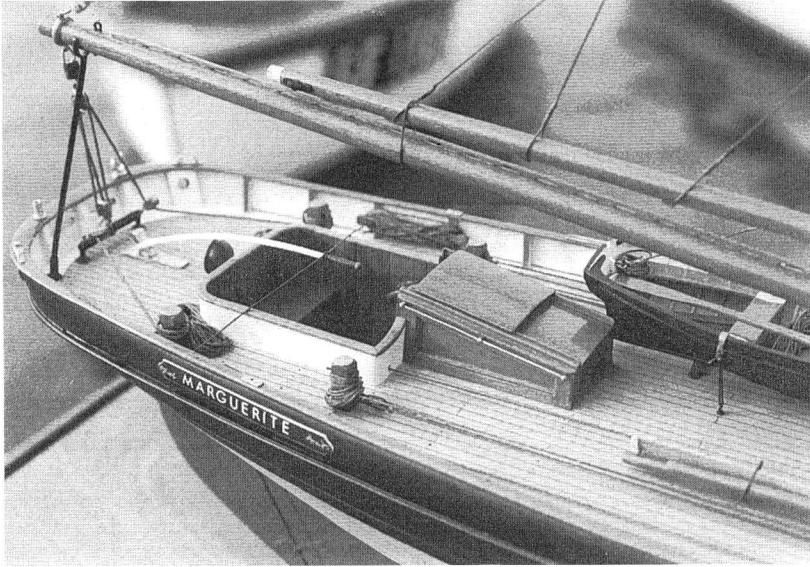

The *Marguerite* by Malcolm Darch. Scale ⅟₃₆th. [courtesy Malcolm
Darch]

The *Marguerite* built for the National Museum of Wales by Kelvin Thatcher. Scale 1":1ft. [courtesy Kelvin Thatcher]

A fine model of the Bristol skiff *Hilda* by Malcolm Darch. Scale ⅜":1ft.
[courtesy Malcolm Darch]

A Swansea Bay pilot schooner.

The Pill skiff *Letty* by retired pilot Syd Dickens. [courtesy John Rich]

A cut-away model of the *Cariad* by Syd Dickens. [courtesy John Rich]

A half-model of the *Petrel* by her builders, Charles Hill & Sons, in 1857. [courtesy Bristol City Museums]

# ACKNOWLEDGEMENTS

In compiling this history I regard myself not so much as author as collator, since it is based largely upon the researches and writings of other historians who have generously put their own work at my disposal.

I am therefore greatly indebted to the following individuals and organisations without whose co-operation this work would not have been possible:

Mr Grahame Farr, upon whose scholarly paper this book is based.

Mr John F. Coates, for allowing me to use his paper on the Swansea Bay Boats.

The late Pilot George Buck of Bristol, and his wife, who so patiently bore my constant interrogations.

Pilot Tom Morgan of Cardiff, for his enthusiastic and knowledgeable encouragement.

Pilot R. Denman of Penarth for allowing me to draw upon his vast technical knowledge.

Pilot 'Billy' Prethero of Barry whose personal recollections were of the greatest value.

Pilots Elvet L. Hare and W. Reed of Port Talbot and Neath for their most valuable assistance.

Messrs Norman and Lewis Alexander for allowing me to use their father's autobiography and collection of photographs, many of which appear in this book.

The late Mr Harold Kimber, shipwright, of Highbridge, for the encouragement and deep constructive interest he has shown throughout this lengthy research and for his constant insistence on accuracy, particularly with regard to the boat construction information.

The late Mr S. Hunt, shipwright, of Pill for his personal recollections.

The late Mr H. Austin of Ilfracombe for his personal recollections as 'man-in-the-boat'.

Pilot J. Morgan of Bristol for the loan of some valuable photographs.

Pilot H.B. Watkins for his generous co-operation in allowing me to use his father's papers.

Mr Ellis of Rangeworthy for permission to use correspondence relating to the dispute at Pill.

The late Mr J. E. Harris of Cardiff for his reminiscences spanning more than seventy years.

174

Capt W. Bartlett of Newport and the magazine *Sea Breezes* for allowing me to use his article on Newport Pilotage.

Pilot T. England, also of Newport.

Mr David Phillips for placing his thesis at my disposal.

Mrs Maurice Buck of Pill for the extracts from James Cox's log-book.

Mr N. Hockley of Barry for his most valuable introductions to various sources of information at Barry and Cardiff.

Mr 'Buller' Brooks of Barry for his personal recollections as 'man-in-the-boat' to various pilots.

The officers of Barry Yacht Club for allowing me to see their club scrap-book and photographs.

Pilot John Rich for arranging many important interviews and obtaining much valuable information.

Mr John Corin for his unfailing constructive support and practical assistance.

The Director of the National Maritime Museum, Greenwich.

The Curator and Staff of the Museum of Wales.

The Staff at the Central Library, Bristol, and the Libraries of Newport, Port Talbot and Barry.

Pilot Morgan of the Gloucester/Sharpness pilotage service.

The Port of Bristol Authority for allowing me to use photographs from their collection.

Ilfracombe Museum for the loan of photographs.

Mr M. Pocock for assistance with photography.

To these and many, many more who have taken the trouble to pass on information, and for the opportunity of meeting so many wonderful people, I am deeply grateful.

Lastly, but by no means least, my thanks to my wife Susan, without whose unswerving strength of purpose, many, many hours of practical assistance with research, interviewing and writing, this work would not have been written, or at least, completed. It is with a sense of the deepest gratitude and the greatest pleasure that I acknowledge her as an equal partner in this enterprise.

P.J.S.
1999

# INDEX

Entries in **bold** relate to illustrations.

176

179

180

# RB Boatbuilding Ltd at the Underfall Yard, Bristol

John Raymond-Barker was bitten by the pilot cutter bug from reading HW Tilman's accounts of sailing ex-Bristol Channel pilot cutters to the furthest-flung corners of the world, experiencing some of the most atrocious conditions. These were old vessels with a lifetime in the pilotage service before being converted to yachts. Tilman lost two of the three pilot cutters he owned, but never – crucially – through stress of weather. They were exceptional vessels built for the dual purpose of sea keeping in the worst weather and the speed to drop off the pilot before the competition could get there.

RB Boatbuilding Ltd is a traditional business, operating out of Bristol's historic city docks, committed to keeping alive the old methods and materials used in constructing these fabulous vessels, which have proved to be very long-lasting and tough, compared to more modern methods.

Researching these vessels and the methods of constructing them, says John R-B, is like a window to the past, and the rich heritage of the Bristol Channel where these vessels were and are built so that they can once more venture out into the Bristol Channel.

The company is dedicated to the re-creation and restoration of classic nineteenth-century, wooden working boats; notably the fast and seaworthy Bristol Channel pilot cutter, widely considered to be among the best sailing boats ever built:

*Mischief*
Photograph courtesy of Ben Punter

The pilot cutter *Morwenna* on the river Avon
Photograph courtesy of Bob Pitchford

'Whether you wish to commission a design for a new and unique vessel or to replicate a historic vessel, we can build you a new craft based on the lines of the Bristol Channel pilot cutters; vessels which have earned an enviable reputation for seaworthiness and performance.

'From various sources there exists an extensive archive of vessel lines worthy of replication. We believe the best of these boats should not be lost to history; we can research your chosen vessel and build a faithful replica, constructed in the same manner as she was originally built.

'We build replicas and new designs of quality and elegance, fast boats with great sea keeping ability, and competitively priced. Our passion is to build boats to cross oceans in.'

*That they fulfilled their function admirably may be guessed when I say that I could find no record of one of those ships being lost through stress of weather.*

*Remember we are speaking of the Bristol Channel in winter. One yachtsman I knew used to take off his hat and keep a moment's silence if anyone mentioned cruising this area in his presence. The gesture was not meant as a joke.*

From: *Messing around in Boats*, by Surgeon Rear-Admiral John R. Muir.

RB Boatbuilding Ltd, Underfall Yard, Cumberland Road, Bristol, BS1 6XG
www.pilotcutter.co.uk